Second Workshop on Advances in Language and Vision Research 2021

Online
11 June 2021

ISBN: 978-1-7138-3014-6

NAACL-HLT 2021

Advances in Language and Vision Research

Proceedings of the Second Workshop

June 11, 2021

Introduction

Language and vision research has attracted great attention from both natural language processing (NLP) and computer vision (CV) researchers. Gradually, this area is shifting from passive perception, templated language and synthetic imagery or environments to active perception, natural language and real-world environments. Thus far, few workshops on language and vision research have been organized by groups from the NLP community. This year, we are organizing the second workshop on Advances in Language and Vision Research (ALVR) in order to promote the frontier of language and vision research and bring interested researchers together to discuss how to best tackle real-world problems in this area.

This workshop covers (but is not limited to) the following topics:

- New tasks and datasets that provide real-world solutions in the intersection of NLP and CV;

- Language-guided interaction with the real world, e.g. navigation via instruction following or dialogue;

- External knowledge integration in visual and language understanding;

- Visually grounded multilingual study, e.g. multimodal machine translation;

- Fairness in multimodal machine learning;

- Shortcoming of existing language and vision tasks and datasets;

- Benefits of using multimodal learning in downstream NLP tasks;

- Self-supervised representation learning in language and vision;

- Transfer learning (including few/zero-shot learning) and domain adaptation;

- Cross-modal learning beyond image understanding, such as videos and audios;

- Multidisciplinary study that may involve linguistics, cognitive science, robotics, etc.

The details of our workshop can be found at `https://alvr-workshop.github.io/`.

Proceedings of the ALVR workshop from previous years can be found on ACL Anthology: `https://www.aclweb.org/anthology/venues/alvr/`

Organizers:

Xin (Eric) Wang, UC Santa Cruz
Ronghang Hu, Facebook AI Research
Drew Hudson, Stanford
Tsu-Jui Fu, UC Santa Barbara
Marcus Rohrbach, Facebook AI Research
Daniel Fried, UC Berkeley

Program Committee:

Shubham Agarwal, Heriot-Watt University
Arjun Akula, University of California, Los Angeles
Asma Ben Abacha, NIH/NLM
Luciana Benotti, The National University of Cordoba
Khyathi Raghavi Chandu, Carnegie Mellon University
Angel Chang, Stanford University
Dhivya Chinnappa, Thomson Reuters
Abhishek Das, Facebook AI
Simon Dobnik, University of Gothenburg
Thoudam Doren Singh, National Institute of Technology, Silchar, India
Hamed Firooz, Facebook AI
Zhe Gan, Microsoft
Cristina Garbacea, University of Michigan
Jack Hessel, AI2
Gabriel Ilharco, University of Washington
Shailza Jolly, TU Kaiserslautern Germany
Marimuthu Kalimuthu, Saarland University, Saarland Informatics Campus
Noriyuki Kojima, Cornell University
Christopher Kummel, Beuth University of Applied Sciences Berlin
Loitongbam Sanayai Meetei, National Institute of Technology Silchar, India
Khanh Nguyen, University of Maryland
Yulei Niu, Renmin University of China
Aishwarya Padmakumar, University of Texas, Austin
Hamid Palangi, Microsoft Research
Shruti Palaskar, Carnegie Mellon University
Vikas Raunak, Carnegie Mellon University
Arka Sadhu, University of Southern California
Alok Singh, National Institute of Technology, Silchar India
Alane Suhr, Cornell University
Hao Tan, University of North Carolina
Xiangru Tang, University of the Chinese Academy of Sciences, China
Ece Takmaz, University of Amsterdam

Invited Speaker:

Jacob Andreas, MIT
Jason Baldridge, Google
Mohit Bansal, UNC Chapel Hill
Yonatan Bisk, Carnegie Mellon University
Joyce Y. Chai, University of Michigan
Yejin Choi, University of Washington

Raymond J. Mooney, University of Texas at Austin
Anna Rohrbach, UC Berkeley
Kate Saenko, Boston University
William Wang, UC Santa Barbara

Table of Contents

Workshop Program

Feature-level Incongruence Reduction for Multimodal Translation
Zhifeng Li, Yu Hong, Yuchen Pan, Jian Tang, Jianmin Yao and Guodong Zhou

Interactive Learning from Activity Description
Khanh Nguyen, Dipendra Misra, Robert Schapire, Miro Dudik and Patrick Shafto

Error Causal inference for Multi-Fusion models
Chengxi Li and Brent Harrison

Leveraging Partial Dependency Trees to Control Image Captions
Wenjie Zhong and Yusuke Miyao

Grounding Plural Phrases: Countering Evaluation Biases by Individuation
Julia Suter, Letitia Parcalabescu and Anette Frank

Towards Multi-Modal Text-Image Retrieval to improve Human Reading
Florian Schneider, Özge Alacam, Xintong Wang and Chris Biemann

PanGEA: The Panoramic Graph Environment Annotation Toolkit
Alexander Ku, Peter Anderson, Jordi Pont Tuset and Jason Baldridge

Learning to Learn Semantic Factors in Heterogeneous Image Classification
Boyue Fan and Zhenting Liu

Reference and coreference in situated dialogue
Sharid Loáiciga, Simon Dobnik and David Schlangen

Language-based Video Editing via Multi-Modal Multi-Level Transformer
Tsu-Jui Fu, Xin Wang, Scott Grafton, Miguel Eckstein and William Yang Wang

Learning to Select Question-Relevant Relations for Visual Question Answering
Hwanhee Lee, Jaewoong Lee, Heejoon Lee and Kyomin Jung

CLEVR_HYP: A Challenge Dataset and Baselines for Visual Question Answering with Hypothetical Actions over Images
Shailaja Keyur Sampat, Akshay Kumar, Yezhou Yang and Chitta Baral

Feature-level Incongruence Reduction for Multimodal Translation

Zhifeng Li, Yu Hong✉**, Yuchen Pan, Jian Tang, Jianmin Yao, Guodong Zhou**
Institute of Artificial Intelligence, Soochow University
School of Computer Science and Technology, Soochow University
No.1, Shizi ST, Suzhou, China, 215006
{lizhifeng0915,tianxianer,yuchenpan59419}@gmail.com
johnnytang1120@gmail.com, {gdzhou,jyao}@suda.edu.cn

Abstract

Caption translation aims to translate image annotations (captions for short). Recently, Multimodal Neural Machine Translation (MNMT) has been explored as the essential solution. Besides of linguistic features in captions, MNMT allows visual (image) featuresto be used. The integration of multimodal features reinforces the semantic representation and considerably improves translation performance. However, MNMT suffers from the incongruence between visual and linguistic features. To overcome the problem, we propose to extend MNMT architecture with a harmonization network, which harmonizes multimodal features (linguistic and visual features) by unidirectional modal space conversion. It enables multimodal translation to be carried out in a seemingly monomodal translation pipeline. We experiment on the golden Multi30k-16 and 17. Experimental results show that, compared to the baseline, the proposed method yields the improvements of 2.2% BLEU for the scenario of translating English captions into German (En→De) at best, 7.6% for the case of English-to-French translation (En→Fr) and 1.5% for English-to-Czech (En→Cz). The utilization of harmonization network leads to the competitive performance to the-state-of-the-art.

1 Introduction

Caption translation is required to translate a source-language caption into target-language, where a caption refers to the sentence-level text annotation of an image. As defined in the shared multimodal translation task[1] in WMT, caption translation can be conducted over both visual features in images and linguistic features of the accompanying captions. The question of how to opportunely utilize images for caption translation motivates the study of multimodality, including not only the extraction of visual features but the cooperation between visual and linguistic features. In this paper, we follow the previous work (Specia et al., 2016) to boil caption translation down to a problem of multimodal machine translation.

So far, a large majority of previous studies tend to develop a neural network based multimodal machine translation model (viz., MNMT), which consists of three basic components:

- **Image encoder** which characterizes a captioned image as a vector of global or multi-regional *visual features* using a convolutional neural network (CNN) (Huang et al., 2016).

- **Neural translation network** (Caglayan et al., 2016; Sutskever et al., 2014; Bahdanau et al., 2014) which serves both to encode a source-language caption and to generate the target-language caption by decoding, where the latent information that flows through the network is referred to *linguistic feature*.

- **Multimodal learning network** which uses visual features to enhance the encoding of linguistic semantics (Ngiam et al., 2011). Besides of the concatenation and combination of linguistic and visual features, vision-to-language attention mechanisms serve as the essential operations for cross-modality learning. Nowadays, they are implemented with single-layer attentive (Caglayan et al., 2017a; Calixto et al., 2017b), doubly-attentive (Calixto et al., 2017a), interpolated (Hitschler et al., 2016) and multi-task (Zhou et al., 2018) neural networks, respectively.

Multimodal learning networks have been successfully grounded with different parts of various neural translation networks. They are proven effective in enhancing translation performance. Nevertheless, the networks suffer from incongruence between visual and linguistic features because:

- Visual and linguistic features are projected into incompatible semantic spaces and therefore fail to be corresponded to each other.

---

[1]http://www.statmt.org/wmt16/

1

Proceedings of the Second Workshop on Advances in Language and Vision Research, pages 1–10

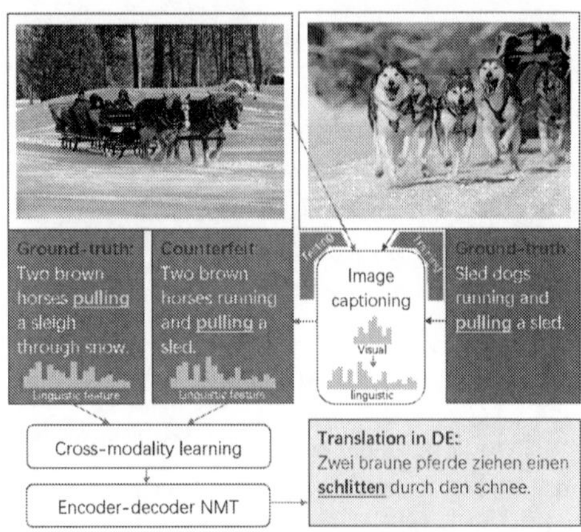

Figure 1: An example in which image captioning contributes to the reduction of incongruence.

- Linguistic features are sequence-dependent. This is attributable to pragmatics, syntax or even rhetoric. On the contrary, visual features are sequence-independent but position-sensitive. This is attributable to spatial relationships of visual elements. Thus, a limited number of visual features can be directly used to improve the understanding of linguistic features and translation.

Considering the Figure 1("*Counterfeit*" means Image Captioning output), the visual features enable a image processing model to recognize "*two horses*" as well as their position relative to a "*sleigh*". However, such features are obscure for a translation model and useful for translating a verb, such as "*pulling*" in the caption. In this case, incongruence of heterogeneous features results from the unawareness of the correspondence between spatial relationship ("*running horses*" ahead of "*sleigh*") and linguistic semantics ("*pulling*").

To ease the incongruence, we propose to equip the current MNMT with a harmonization network, in which visual features are not directly introduced into the encoding of linguistic semantics. Instead, they are transformed into linguistic features before absorbed into semantic representations. In other words, we tend to make a detour during the cross-modality understanding, so as to bypass the modality barrier (Figure 2). In our experiments, we employ a captioning model to conduct harmonization. The hidden states it produced for decoding caption words are intercepted and involved into the representation learning process of MNMT.

The rest of the paper is organized as follows: Section 2 presents the motivation and methodolog-

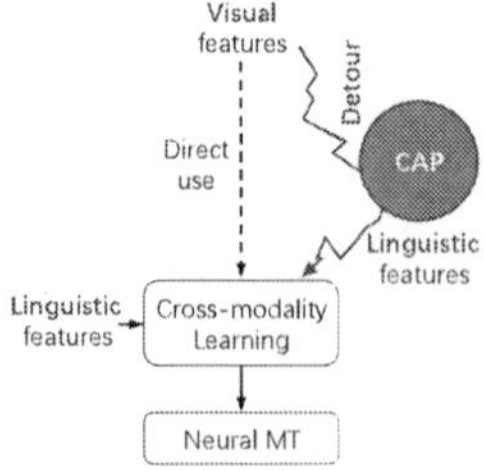

Figure 2: Bypassing modality barrier by captioning.

ical framework. Section 3 gives the NMT model we use. In Section 4, we introduce the captioning model that is trainable for cross-modality feature space transformation. Section 5 presents the captioning based harmonization networks as well as the resultant MNMT models. We discuss test results in Section 6 and overview the related work in Section 7. We conclude the paper in section 8.

2 Fundamentals and Methodological Framework

We utilize Anderson et al (2018)'s image captioning (CAP for short) to guide the cross-modality feature transformation, converting visual features into linguistic. CAP is one of the generation models which are specially trained to generate language conditioned on visual features of images. Ideally, during training, it learns to perceive the correspondence between visual and linguistic features, such as that between the spatial relationship of "*running dogs ahead of a sled*" in Figure 1 and the meaning of the verb "*pulling*". This allows CAP to produce appropriate linguistic features during testing in terms of similar visual features, such as that in the case of predicting the verb "*pulling*" for the scenario of "*running horses ahead of a sleigh*".

Methodologically speaking, we adopt the linguistic features produced by the encoder of CAP instead of the captions generated by the decoder of CAP. On the basis, we integrate both the linguistic features of the original source-language caption and those produced by CAP into Calixto et al (2017b)'s attention-based cross-modality learning model (see Figure 3). Experimenal results show that the learning model substantially improves Bahdanau et al (2014)'s encoder-decoder NMT system.

3 Preliminary 1: Attentive Encoder-Decoder NMT (Baseline)

We take Bahdanau et al. (2014)'s attentive encoder-decoder NMT as the baseline. It is constructed

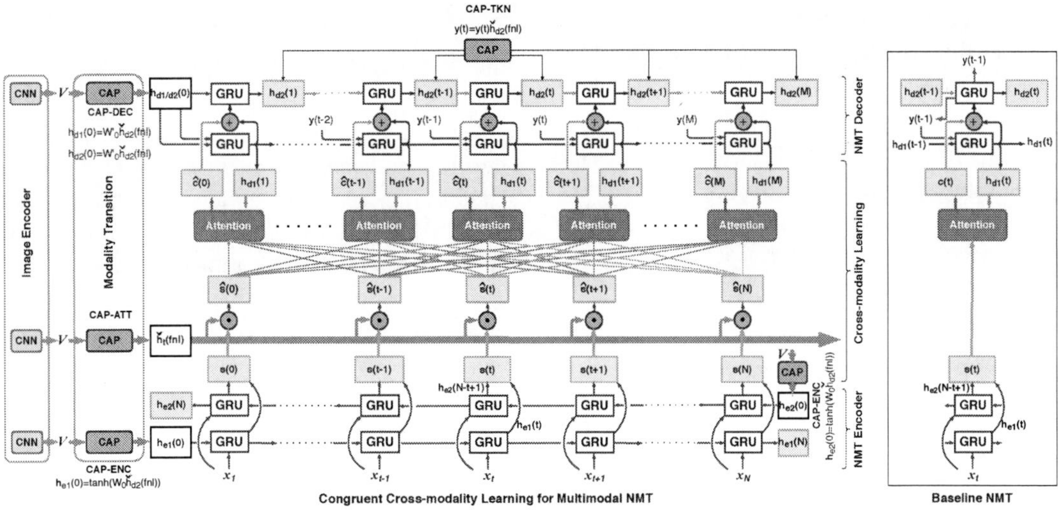

Figure 3: The overall architecture of MNMT.

with a BiGRU encoder and a Conditional GRU (CGRU) decoder (Firat and Cho, 2016; Caglayan et al., 2017a). Attention mechanism is used between BiGRU and CGRU. The diagram at the right side of Figure 3 shows the baseline framework.

For a source-language caption, we represent it with a sequence of randomly-initialized (Kalchbrenner and Blunsom, 2013) word embeddings $X=(x_1, ..., x_N)$, where each x_t is uniformly specified as a k-dimensional word embedding. Conditioned on the embeddings, Chung et al (2014)'s BiGRU is used to compute the bidirectional hidden states $S=(s_1, ..., s_N)$, where each s_t is obtained by combining the t-th hidden state of forward GRU and that of backward GRU: $s_t=[\overrightarrow{GRU}^e(x_t), \overleftarrow{GRU}^e(x_t)]$. Padding (Libovický and Helcl, 2018) and dynamic stabilization (Ba et al., 2016) are used.

Firat and Cho (2016)'s CGRU is utilized for decoding, which comprises two forward GRU units, i.e., $\overrightarrow{GRU}^{d1}$ and $\overrightarrow{GRU}^{d2}$ respectively. $\overrightarrow{GRU}^{d1}$ plays the role of producing the inattentive decoder hidden states $H^{d1}=(h_1^{d1}, ..., h_M^{d1})$, where each h_t^{d1} is computed based on the output state h_{t-1}^{d1} and prediction y_{t-1} at the previous time step: $h_t^{d1}=\overrightarrow{GRU}^{d1}(h_{t-1}^{d1}, y_{t-1})$ (Note: the prediction y_t denotes the k-dimensional embedding of the predicted word at the t-th decoding step). By contrast, $\overrightarrow{GRU}^{d2}$ serves to produce the attentive decoder hidden states $H^{d2}=(h_1^{d2}, ..., h_M^{d2})$, where each h_t^{d2} is computed conditioned on the previous attentive state h_{t-1}^{d2}, the current inattentive state h_t^{d1}, as well as the current attention-aware context c_t:

$h_t^{d2}=\overrightarrow{GRU}^{d2}(h_{t-1}^{d2}, h_t^{d1} \oplus c_t)$. The context c_t is obtained by the attention mechanism over the global encoder hidden states S: $c_t = \alpha_t S$, where α_t denotes the attention weight at the t-th time step. Eventually, the prediction of each target-language word is carried out as follows (where, W_h, W_c, W_y, b_o and b_y are trainable parameters):

$$\mathcal{D}_t(y_{t-1}, h_t^{d2}, c_t) \sim \begin{cases} o_t = tanh(y_{t-1} + W_h h_t^{d2} + \\ \quad W_c c_t + b_o) \\ P(y_t|o_t) = \text{softmax}(W_y^\top o_t \\ \quad + b_y) \end{cases}$$
$$(1)$$

4 Preliminary 2: Image-dependent Linguistic Feature Acquisition by CAP

For an image, captioning models serve to generate a sequence of natural language (caption) that describes the image. Such kind of models are capable of transforming visual features into linguistic features by encoder-decoder networks. We utilize Anderson et al. (2018)'s CAP to obtain the transformed linguistic features.

4.1 CNN based Image Encoder

What we feed into CAP is a full-size image which needs to be convolutionally encoded beforehand. He et al (He et al., 2016a)'s CNNs (known as ResNet) with deep residual learning mechanism (He et al., 2016b) is capable of encoding images. In our experiments, we employ the recent version

3

of ResNet, i.e., ResNet-101 , which is constructed with 101 convolutional layers. It is pretrained on ImageNet (Russakovsky et al., 2015) in the scenario of 1000-class image classification.

Using ResNet-101, we characterize an image as a convolutional feature matrix: $V \in \mathbb{R}^{k \times 2048} = \{v_1, ..., v_k\}$, in which each element $v_i \in \mathbb{R}^{2048}$ is a real-valued vector and corresponds to an image region in the size of 14×14 pixels.

4.2 Top-down Attention-based CAP

CAP learns to generate a caption over V. It is constructed with two-layer RNNs with LSTM (Anderson et al., 2018), LSTM1 and LSTM2 respectively. LSTM1 (in layer-1) computes the current first-layer hidden state $\check{h}_t^{d1}$ conditioned on the current first-layer input $\check{x}_t^{d1}$ and previous hidden state $\check{h}_{t-1}^{d1}$: $\check{h}_t^{d1}$=LSTM1($\check{x}_t^{d1}, \check{h}_{t-1}^{d1}$). The input $\check{x}_t^{d1}$ is obtained by concatenating the previous hidden state $\check{h}_{t-1}^{d1}$ and previous prediction $\check{y}_{t-1}$, as well as the condensed global visual feature $\bar{v}$: $\check{x}_t^{d1}$=[$\bar{v}, \check{h}_{t-1}^{d1}, \check{y}_{t-1}$], where $\bar{v}$ is calculated by the normalized accumulation of overall convolutional features in V: $\bar{v} = \frac{1}{k} \sum_i v_i \, (\forall v_i \in V)$. We specify the first-layer hidden state as the initial image-dependent linguistic features.

Attention mechanism (Sennrich et al., 2015) is used for highlighting the attention-worthy image context, so as to produce the attention-aware vector of image context $\check{v}_t$: $\check{v}_t = \sum \check{\alpha}_t V$. The attention weight $\check{\alpha}_t$ is obtained by aligning the current image-dependent hidden state $\check{h}_t^{d1}$ with every convoluted visual feature v_i: $\check{\alpha}_t = \text{softmax}(f(\check{h}_t^{d1}, v_i))$, where $f(*)$ is the non-linear activation function.

LSTM2 (in layer-2) serves as a neural language model (viz., language-oriented generation model). It learns to encode the current second-layer hidden state $\check{h}_t^{d2}$ conditioned on the current second-layer input $\check{x}_t^{d2}$ and previous hidden state $\check{h}_{t-1}^{d2}$: $\check{h}_t^{d2}$=LSTM2($\check{x}_t^{d2}, \check{h}_{t-1}^{d2}$). The input $\check{x}_t^{d2}$ is obtained by concatenating the current first-layer hidden state $\check{h}_t^{d1}$ (emitted from layer-1) and current attention-aware image context $\check{v}_t$: $\check{x}_t^{d2}$=[$\check{v}_t, \check{h}_t^{d1}$]. We specific a second-layer hidden state $\check{h}_t^{d2}$ as the image-dependent attention-aware linguistic features. Towards the image captioning task, CAP generally decodes the second-layer hidden states $\check{h}_t^{d2}$ to predict caption words. In our case, we tend to integrate them into multimodal NMT by cross-modality learning (see the next section).

5 Harmonization for MNMT

In the previous work of multimodal NMT, visual features in V are directly used for cross-modality learning. By contrast, we transform visual features into image-dependent attention-aware linguistic features (i.e., second-layer hidden states $\check{h}_t^{d2}$ emitted by CAP) before use. We provide four-class variants of cross-modality learning to improve NMT. They absorb image-dependent attention-aware linguistic features in different ways, including a variant that comprises attentive feature fusion (CAP-ATT) and three variants (CAP-ENC, CAP-DEC and CAP-TKN) which carry out reinitialization and target-language embedding modulation. Figure 3 shows the positions in the baseline NMT where the variants come into play.

CAP-ATT intends to improve NMT by conducting joint representation learning across the features of the source-language caption and that of the accompanying image. On one side, CAP-ATT adopts the encoder hidden state s_t (emitted by the Bi-GRU encoder of the baseline NMT) and uses it as the language-dependent linguistic feature. On the other side, it takes the image-dependent attention-aware linguistic feature $\check{h}_t^{d2}$ (produced by CAP). We suppose that the two kinds of features (i.e., $\check{h}_t^{d2}$ and s_t) are congruent with each other. On the basis, CAP-ATT blends $\check{h}_t^{d2}$ into s_t to form the joint representation $\widehat{s}_t$. Element-wise feature fusion (Cao and Xiong, 2018) is used to compute $\widehat{s}_t$: $\widehat{s}_t = s_t \odot \check{h}_t^{d2}$. Using the joint representation $\widehat{s}_t$, CAP-ATT updates the attention-aware context c_t which is fed into the CGRU decoder of the baseline NMT: $\widehat{c}_t = \alpha_t \widehat{S}, \; \forall \widehat{s} \in \widehat{S}$. By substituting the updated context $\widehat{c}_t$ into the computation of the CGRU decoder, CAP-ATT further refines the decoder hidden state $h_t^{d_2}$ and prediction of target-language words. Equation 2 formulates the decoding process, where $\mathcal{D}_t$ is the shorthand of equation (1).

$$\widehat{\mathcal{D}}_t(y_{t-1}, \widehat{h}_t^{d2}, \widehat{c}_t) \sim \begin{cases} \widehat{h}_t^{d_2} = \overrightarrow{GRU}^{d2}(\widehat{h}_{t-1}^{d_2}, h_t^{d_1} \\ \qquad \oplus \widehat{c}_t) \\ y_t \Leftarrow \mathcal{D}_t(y_{t-1}, \widehat{h}_t^{d_2}, c_t) \end{cases}$$

$$(2)$$

CAP-ENC reinitializes the BiGRU encoder of the baseline NMT with the final image-dependent attention-aware linguistic feature $\check{h}_t^{d2}$ (t=N) (produced by CAP): $\overleftarrow{h}_0 = \overrightarrow{h}_0 = \tanh(W_0 \check{h}_t^{d2})$, where $\overleftarrow{h}_0$ and $\overrightarrow{h}_0$ are the initial states of BiGRU, and W_0 refers to the trainable parameter. **CAP-**

DEC uses $\check{h}_t^{d2}$ ($t{=}N$) to reinitialize the CGRU decoder of the baseline NMT: $h_0^{d1} = h_0^{d2} = \tanh(W_0' \check{h}_t^{d2})$, where h_0^{d1} and h_0^{d2} are the initial decoder hidden states of CGRU. **CAP-TKN** modulates the predicted target-language word embedding y_t with $\check{h}_t^{d2}$ ($t{=}N$) at each decoding step: $y_t = y_t \odot \tanh(W_{tkn} \check{h}_t^{d2})$, where W_{tkn} is the trainable parameter. **CAP-ALL** equips a MNMT system with all the variants.

6 Experimentation

6.1 Resource and Experimental Datasets

We perform experiments on Multi30k-16 and Multi30k-17[2], which are provided by WMT for the shared tasks of multilingual captioning and multimodal MT (Elliott et al., 2016). The corpora are used as the extended versions of Flichr30k (Young et al., 2014), since they contain not only English (En) image captions but their translations in German (De), French (Fr) and Czech (Cz). Hereinafter, we specify an example in Multi30k as an image which is accompanied by three En→De, En→Fr and En→Cz caption-translation pairs. Each of Multi30k-*16* and Multi30k-*17* contains about 31K examples. We experiment on the corpora separately, and as usual divide each of them into training, validation and test sets, at the scale of 29K, 1,014 and 1K examples, respectively.

In addition, we carry out a complementary experiment on the ambiguous COCO which contains 461 examples (Elliott et al., 2017). Due to the inclusion of ambiguous verbs, the examples in ambiguous COCO can be used for the evaluation of visual sense disambiguation in a MNMT scenario.

6.2 Training and Hyperparameter Settings

For preprocessing, we apply Byte-Pair Encoding (BPE) (Sennrich et al., 2015) for tokenizing all the captions and translations in Multi30k and COCO, and use the open-source toolkit[3] of Moses (Koehn et al., 2007) for lowercasing and punctuation normalization. It reproduces the neural network architecture of Anderson et al (Anderson et al., 2018)'s top-down attentive CAP. The only difference is that it merely utilizes ResNet-101 in generating the input set of visual features V, without the use of Faster R-CNN (Ren et al., 2015). This CAP has

been trained on MSCOCO captions dataset (Lin et al., 2014) using the same hyperparameter settings as that in Anderson et al. (2018)'s work.

Besides of the baseline NMT (Bahdanau et al., 2014) mentioned in section 2, we compare our model with Caglayan et al (Caglayan et al., 2017a)'s convolutional visualfeature based MNMT. In this paper, we follow Caglayan et al (Caglayan et al., 2017a)'s practice to implement and train our model. First of all, we implement our model with the nmtpy framework (Caglayan et al., 2017b) using Theano v0.9. During training, ADAM with a learning rate of 4e-4 is used and the batch size is set as 32. We initialize all the parameters (i.e., transformation matrices and biases) using Xavier and clip the total gradient norm to 5. We drop out the input embeddings, hidden states and output states with the probabilities of (0.3, 0.5, 0.5) for En→De MT, (0.2, 0.4, 0.4) for En→Fr and (0.1, 0.3, 0.3) for En→Cz. In order to avoid overfitting, we apply a L_2 regularization term with a factor of $1e$-5. We specify the dimension as 128 for all token embeddings ($k = 128$) and 256 for hidden states.

6.3 Comparison to the Baseline

We carry out 5 independent experiments (5 runs) for each of the proposed MNMT variants. In each run, any of the variants is retrained and redeveloped under cold-start conditions using a set of randomly-selected seeds by MultEval[4]. Eventually, the resultant models are evaluated on the test set with BLEU (Papineni et al., 2002), METEOR (Denkowski and Lavie, 2014) and TER (Snover et al., 2006).

For each variant, we report not only the comprehensive performance (denoted as $ensemble$) which is obtained using ensemble learning (Garmash and Monz, 2016) but that without ensemble learning. In the latter case, the average performance (μ) and deviations (σ) in the 5 runs are reported.

6.3.1 Performance on Multi30k

Tables 1 and 2 respectively show the performance of our models on Multi30k-16 and Multi30k-17 for the translation scenarios of En→De, En→Fr and En→Cz. Each of our MNMT models in the tables is denoted with a symbol "+", which indicates that a MNMT model is constructed with the baseline and one of our cross-modality learning models. The baseline is specified as the monomodal NMT model which is developed by Bahdanau et al. (2014) (as

---

[2]https://github.com/multi30k/dataset/tree/master/data-/task1/raw

[3]https://github.com/moses-smt/mosesdecoder/tree/-master/scripts/tokenizer

[4]https://github.com/jhclark/multeval

En→De	Multi30k-*16* ($\mu \pm \sigma$/ensemble)			Multi30k-*17* ($\mu \pm \sigma$/ensemble)		
	BLEU	METEOR	TER	BLEU	METEOR	TER
Baseline	38.1±0.8/40.7	57.3±0.5/59.2	N/A	30.8±1.0/33.7	51.6±0.5/53.8	N/A
+CAP−ATT	39.2±0.8/41.3	57.5±0.6/59.4	40.9±0.8/39.5	32.1±0.9/33.6	51.0±0.7/52.9	48.7±0.8/47.3
+CAP−ENC	39.1±0.8/41.2	57.6±0.7/59.2	40.9±0.8/39.3	32.5±0.8/33.8	**52.2±0.7/54.5**	**48.5±0.8/46.3**
+CAP−DEC	38.9±0.8/41.0	57.4±0.7/59.3	**41.3±0.8/39.1**	**33.0±0.8/34.3**	51.6±0.7/53.2	48.6±0.8/47.1
+CAP−TKN	39.1±0.8/40.9	57.3±0.6/58.6	**41.3±0.8/39.1**	32.2±0.8/33.9	51.3±0.7/53.5	48.5±0.8/47.0
+CAP−ALL	**39.6±0.9/42.1**	**57.5±0.7/59.9**	41.1±0.8/39.4	31.6±0.8/33.9	51.6±0.7/53.7	49.7±0.7/47.1
En→Fr	Multi30k-*16* ($\mu \pm \sigma$/ensemble)			Multi30k-*17* ($\mu \pm \sigma$/ensemble)		
	BLEU	METEOR	TER	BLEU	METEOR	TER
Baseline	52.5±0.3/54.3	69.6±0.1/71.3	N/A	50.4±0.9/53.0	67.5±0.7/69.8	N/A
+CAP−ATT	**60.1±0.8/63.3**	**74.3±0.6/77.1**	**25.1±0.7/22.7**	52.5±0.9/56.1	68.2±0.7/71.2	31.5±0.7/28.4
+CAP−ENC	59.3±0.9/62.8	73.5±0.6/76.4	26.2±0.7/23.3	52.2±0.8/55.8	68.1±0.7/71.1	31.5±0.7/28.5
+CAP−DEC	60.1±0.9/62.6	74.2±0.7/76.3	25.6±0.6/23.0	51.9±0.9/55.7	67.6±0.7/71.3	**31.6±0.7/28.1**
+CAP−TKN	60.3±0.8/63.0	74.5±0.6/76.6	25.2±0.6/23.0	52.7±0.9/56.0	**68.3±0.6/71.3**	31.5±0.7/28.6
+CAP−ALL	60.1±0.8/62.7	74.3±0.6/76.4	25.0±0.4/23.1	**52.8±0.9/56.1**	68.6±0.6/71.1	31.2±0.7/28.9

Table 1: Performance for both En→De and En→Fr on Multi30k-16 and Multi30k-17.

En→Cz	Multi30k(2016) ($\mu \pm \sigma$ /ensemble)		
	BLEU	METEOR	TER
Baseline	30.5±0.8/32.6	29.3±0.4/31.4	N/A
+CAP−ATT	31.8±0.9/33.4	**30.2±0.4/32.6**	46.1±0.8/43.6
+CAP−ENC	31.7±0.8/33.3	29.9±0.4/32.1	46.3±0.8/43.5
+CAP−DEC	31.6±0.9/33.3	30.0±0.4/32.3	45.6±0.8/43.6
+CAP−TKN	**32.0±0.9/33.9**	30.1±0.4/32.3	45.7±0.8/43.3
+CAP−ALL	31.8±0.9/33.6	29.9±0.4/31.5	**45.3±0.8/43.3**

Table 2: Performance for En→Cz on Multi30k-16

mentioned in section 2) and redeveloped as the baselines in a variety of research studies on multimodal NMT (Calixto et al., 2017a,b; Caglayan et al., 2017a). We quote the results reported in Caglayan et al. (2017a)'s work as they were better.

It can be observed that our MNMT models outperform the baseline. They benefits from the performance gains yielded by the variants of CAP based cross-modality learning, which are no less than 1.5% BLEU when ensemble learning is used, and 0.6% when not to use it. In particular, +CAP-ATT obtains a performance increase of up to 7.6% BLEU (μ) in the scenario of En→Fr MT. The gains in METEOR score we obtain are less obvious than that in BLEU, which is about 5.3% (μ) at best.

We follow Clark et al. (2011) to perform significance test. The test results show that +CAP-ATT, +CAP-DEC and +CAP-TKN achieve a p-value of 0.02, 0.01 and 0.007, respectively. Clark et al. (2011) have proven that the performance improvements are significant only if the p-value is less than 0.05. Therefore, the proposed method yields statistically significant performance gains.

6.3.2 Performance on Ambiguous COCO

Table 3 shows the translation performance. It can be found that our models yield a certain amount of gains (in BLEU scores) for En→De translation, and raise both BLEU and METEOR scores for En→Fr.

The METER scores for En→De are comparable to that the baseline achieved. However, the improvement is less significant compared to that obtained on Multi30k-16&17 (see Table 1). Considering that the ambiguous COCO contains a larger number of ambiguous words than Multi30k-16&17, we suggest that our method fails to largely shield the baseline from the misleading of ambiguous words.

Nevertheless, our method doesn't result in a twofold error propagation, but on the contrary it alleviates the negative influences of the errors because:

- Error propagation, in general, is inevitable when a GRU or LSTM unit is used. Both are trained to predict a sequence of words one by one. Appropriate prediction of previous words is crucial for ensuring the correctness of subsequent words. Thus, once a mistake is made at a certain decoding step, the error will be propagated forward, and mislead the prediction of subsequent words.

- The baseline is equipped with a GRU decoder and therefore suffers from error propagation. More seriously, ambiguous words increase the risk of error propagation. This causes a significant performance reduction on Ambiguous COCO. For example, the BLEU score for En→De is 28.7% at best. It is far below that (40.7%) obtained on Multi30k-16&17.

- Two-fold error propagation is suspected to occur when LSTM-based CAP is integrated with the baseline. Though the opposite is actually true. After CAP is used, the translation performance is improved instead of falling down.

6.4 Comparison to the state of the art

We survey the state-of-the-art research activities in the field of MNMT, and compare them with ours

Ambiguous	En→De ($\mu \pm \sigma$/ensemble)			En→Fr ($\mu \pm \sigma$/ensemble)		
coco (2017)	BLEU	METEOR	TER	BLEU	METEOR	TER
Helcl et al (2017)	25.7	45.6	N/A	43.0	62.5	N/A
Caglayan et al (2017)	29.4$^\diamond$	49.2$^\diamond$	N/A	46.2$^\diamond$	66.0$^\diamond$	N/A
Zhou et al (2018)	28.3	48.0	N/A	45.0	64.7	N/A
Baseline	26.4±0.2/28.7	46.8±0.7/48.9	N/A	41.2±1.2/43.3	61.3±0.9/63.3	N/A
+CAP-ATT	27.1±1.2/29.3	47.7±0.9/48.8	**53.0±1.1/50.7**	43.8±1.2/46.8	62.2±0.9/65.0	36.5±1.0/34.5
+CAP-ENC	27.1±1.1/29.4	47.5±0.9/48.7	54.1±1.1/51.2	42.8±1.2/46.3	60.8±0.9/65.3	**38.1±1.0/33.4**
+CAP-DEC	**27.8±1.1/29.9**	**47.8±1.0/49.3**	53.8±1.1/50.8	43.2±1.2/46.1	61.5±0.9/65.3	37.3±1.0/34.3
+CAP-TKN	27.3±1.2/29.6	46.4±0.9/48.9	54.2±1.2/51.1	44.5±1.2/46.8	62.4±0.9/65.3	37.8±1.0/34.0
+CAP-ALL	27.6±1.1/29.8	46.4±0.9/48.9	54.4±1.2/50.8	**44.3±1.2/47.1**	**62.6±0.9/65.4**	36.4±1.0/33.5

Table 3: Performance on Amb-COCO (Note: "$\diamond$" is the sign of the performance when ensemble learning is used.)

En→De	Multi30k-*16*		Multi30k-*17*	
	BLEU	METEOR	BLEU	METEOR
Huang et al (2016)	36.5	54.1		
Calixto et al (2017a)	36.5	55.0		
Calixto et al (2017b)	41.3$^\diamond$	59.2$^\diamond$		
Elliott et al (2017)	40.2$^\diamond$	59.3$^\diamond$		
Helcl et al (2017)	34.6	51.7	28.5	49.2
Caglayan et al (2017a)	41.2$^\diamond$	59.4$^\diamond$	33.5$^\diamond$	53.8$^\diamond$
Helcl et al (2018)	38.7	57.2		
Zhou et al (2018)			31.6	52.2
Ours (μ)	39.6	57.5	33.0	52.2
Ours (ensemble)	**42.1**	**59.9**	**34.3**	**54.5**
En→Fr	Multi30k-*16*		Multi30k-*17*	
	BLEU	METEOR	BLEU	METEOR
Helcl et al (2017)			50.3	67.0
Caglayan et al (2017a)	56.7$^\diamond$	73.0$^\diamond$	55.7$^\diamond$	71.9$^\diamond$
Helcl et al (2018)	60.8	75.1		
Zhou et al (2018)			53.8	70.3
Ours (μ)	60.1	74.3	52.8	68.6
Ours (ensemble)	**63.3**	**77.1**	**56.1**	**71.1**
En→Cz	Multi30k-*16*		Multi30k-*17*	
	BLEU	METEOR	BLEU	METEOR
Helcl et al (2018)	31.0	29.9		
Ours (μ)	32.0	30.2		
Ours (ensemble)	**33.9**	**32.6**		

Table 4: Comparison results on Multi30k (Note: "$\diamond$" is the sign indicating the use of ensemble learning).

(as shown in Table 4). Comparison are made for all the WMT translation scenarios (En→De, Fr and Cz) on Multi30k-16&17 but merely for En→De and En→Fr on ambiguous COCO (as shown in Table 3). To our best knowledge, there is no previous attempt to evaluate the performance of an En→Cz translation model on ambiguous COCO, and thus a precise comparison for that is not available. It is noteworthy that some of the cited work reports the ensemble learning results for MNMT, others make no mention of it. We label the former with a symbol of "$\diamond$" in Tables 3 and 4 to ease the comparison.

It can be observed that our best model outperforms the state of the art for most scenarios over different corpora except the En→Fr case on Multi30k-17. The performance increases are most apparent in the case of En→Fr on Multi30k-16 when ensemble learning is used, where the BLEU and METEOR scores reach the levels of more than 63% and 77%, with the improvements of 6.6% and 4.1%.

We regard the work of Caglayan et al. (2017a)

and Calixto et al. (2017a) as the representatives in our systematic analysis. Caglayan et al. (2017a) directly use raw visual features (i.e., V mentioned in section 3.1) to enhance NMT at different stages, including that of initialization, encoding and decoding. Calixto et al. (2017a) develop a doubly-attentive decoder, where both visual features of images and linguistic features of captions are used for computing the attention scores during decoding.

- **Caglayan et al. (2017a)'s model**: Caglayan et al. (2017a)'s model integrates visual features V into the decoding process. By contrast, we conduct the integration using linguistic features which are transformed from visual features. It is proven that our integration approach leads to considerable performance increases. Accordingly, we suppose that reducing incongruence between visual and linguistic features contributes to cross-modality learning in MNMT.

- **Calixto et al. (2017a)'s model**: Our CAP-ATT is similar to Calixto et al. (2017a)'s model due to the use of attention mechanisms during decoding. The difference is that CAP-ATT transforms visual features into linguistic features before attention computation. This operation leads to the increases of both BLEU (2.7%) and METEOR (2%) on Multi30k-16. The results demonstrate that attention scores can be computed more effectively between features of the same type.

6.5 Performance in Adversarial Evaluation

We examine the use efficiency of images for MNMT using Elliott's adversarial evaluation (Elliott, 2018). Elliott suppose that if a model efficiently uses images during MNMT, its performance would degrade when it is cheated by some incongruent images. Table 5 shows the test results, where "C" is specified as a METEOR score which is evaluated when there is not any incongruent image in the test set, while "I" is that when some incongruent images are used to replace the original images.

If the value of "C" is larger than "I", a positive $\triangle_E$-Awareness can be obtained. It illustrates an acceptable use efficiency. On the contrary, a negative $\triangle_E$-Awareness is a warning of low efficiency.

Table 5 shows the test results. It can be observed that our +CAP-ATT and +CAP-ALL models achieve positive $\triangle_E$-Awareness for all the translation scenarios on Multi30k-16. In addition, the models obtain higher values of $\triangle_E$-Awareness than Caglayan et al. (2017a)'s models of `decinit` and `hierattn`. As mentioned above, Caglayan et al directly use visual features to enhance the MNMT, while we use the image-dependent linguistic features that are transformed from visual features. Therefore, we suppose that modality transformation leads to a higher use efficiency of images.

7 RELATED WORK

We have mentioned the previous work of MNMT in section 1, where the research interest has been classified into image encoding, encoder-decoder NMT construction and cross-modality learning. Besides, we present the methods of Caglayan et al. (2017a) and Calixto et al. (2017a) in the section 4.4.2, along with the systematic analysis. Besides, many scholars within the research community have made great efforts upon the development of sophisticated NMT architectures, including multi-source (Zoph and Knight, 2016), multi-task (Dong et al., 2015) and multi-way (Firat et al., 2016) NMT, as well as those equipped with attention mechanisms (Sennrich et al., 2015). The research activities are particularly crucial since they broaden the range of cross-modality learning strategies.

Current research interest has concentrated on the incorporation of visual features into NMT (Lala et al., 2018), by means of visual-linguistic context vector concatenation (Libovický et al., 2016), doubly-attentive decoding (Calixto et al., 2017a), hierarchical attention combination (Libovický and Helcl, 2017), cross-attention network (Helcl et al., 2018), gated attention network (Zhang et al., 2019), joint (Zhou et al., 2018) and ensemble (Zheng et al., 2018) learning . In addition, image attention optimization (Delbrouck and Dupont, 2017) and monolingual data expansion (Hitschler et al., 2016) have been proven effective in this field. Ive et al. (2019) use an off-shelf object detector and an additional image dataset (Kuznetsova et al., 2018) to form a bag of category-level object embeddings. Conditioned on the embeddings, Ive et al. (2019) develop

En→De	Multi30k (2016) ($\mu \pm \sigma$)		
	C	I	$\triangle_E$-Awareness
+CAP-ATT	58.5	58.5±0.2	0.001 ±0.002
+CAP-ENC	57.8	58.5±0.1	-0.007 ±0.001
+CAP-DEC	58.3	58.0±0.0	0.020 ±0.001
+CAP-TKN	58.7	58.6±0.1	0.001 ±0.001
+CAP-ALL	**59.0**	**58.5±0.2**	**0.005 ±0.002**
Caglayan et al's trgmul	N/A	N/A	-0.001 ±0.002
Caglayan et al's decinit	N/A	N/A	0.003 ±0.001
Helcl et al's hierattn	N/A	N/A	0.019 ±0.003

En→Fr	Multi30k (2016) ($\mu \pm \sigma$)		
	C	I	$\triangle_E$-Awareness
+CAP-ATT	**74.8**	**74.2±0.1**	**0.005 ±0.001**
+CAP-ENC	73.8	74.2±0.1	-0.004 ±0.001
+CAP-DEC	74.3	74.3±0.1	-0.001 ±0.001
+CAP-TKN	74.9	74.6±0.1	0.003 ±0.001
+CAP-ALL	74.8	74.5±0.1	0.003 ±0.001

En→Cz	Multi30k (2016) ($\mu \pm \sigma$)		
	C	I	$\triangle_E$-Awareness
+CAP-ATT	35.2	34.7±0.2	0.005 ±0.002
+CAP-ENC	34.7	34.4±0.1	0.003 ±0.001
+CAP-DEC	34.8	34.4±0.1	0.004 ±0.001
+CAP-TKN	34.9	35.1±0.1	-0.002 ±0.001
+CAP-ALL	**34.6**	**33.8±0.1**	**0.007 ±0.001**

Table 5: Test results in Elliott's utility test.

a sophisticated MNMT model which integrates self-attention and cross-attention mechanisms into the encoder-decoder based deliberation architecture.

This paper also touches on the research area of image captioning. Mao et al. (2014) provide an interpretable image modeling method using multimodal RNN. Vinyals et al. (2015) design a caption generator (IDG) by Seq2Seq framework. Further, Xu et al. (2015) propose an attention-based IDG.

8 CONCLUSION

We demonstrate that the captioning based harmonization model reduces incongruence between multimodal features. This contributes to the performance improvement of MNMT. It is proven that our method increases the use efficiency of images.

The interesting phenomenon we observed in the experiments is that modality incongruence reduction is more effective in the scenario of En→Fr translation than that of En→De and En→Cz. This raises a problem of adaptation to languges. In the future, we will study on the distinct grammatical and syntactic principles of target languages, as well as their influences on the adaptation. For example, the syntax of French can be considered as most strict. Thus, a sequence-dependent feature vector may be more adaptive to MNMT towards French. Accordingly, we will attempt to develop a generative adversarial network based adaptation enhancement model. The goal is to refine the generated linguistic features by learning to detect and eliminate the features of less adaptability.

Acknowledgements

We thank the reviewers for their insightful comments. The idea is proposed by the corresponding author (Yu Hong). Jian Tang provides an effective assistance for conducting the experiments. We thank the colleagues for their help.

This work was supported by the national Natural Science Foundation of China (NSFC) via Grant Nos. 62076174, 61773276, 61836007.

References

P. Anderson, X. He, C. Buehler, D. Teney, M. Johnson, S. Gould, and L. Zhang. 2018. Bottom-up and top-down attention for image captioning and visual question answering. In *CVPR*, volume 3, page 6.

J. L. Ba, J. R. Kiros, and G. E. Hinton. 2016. Layer normalization. *arXiv:1607.06450*.

D. Bahdanau, K. Cho, and Y. Bengio. 2014. Neural machine translation by jointly learning to align and translate. *arXiv:149.0473*.

O. Caglayan, W. Aransa, A. Bardet, M. García-Martínez, F. Bougares, L. Barrault, M. Masana, L. Herranz, and J. Van de Weijer. 2017a. Lium-cvc submissions for wmt17 multimodal translation task. pages 450–457.

O. Caglayan, W. Aransa, Y. Wang, M. Masana, M. García-Martínez, F. Bougares, L. Barrault, and J. Van de Weijer. 2016. Does multimodality help human and machine for translation and image captioning? *arXiv:1605.09186*.

O. Caglayan, M. García-Martínez, A. Bardet, W. Aransa, F. Bougares, and L. Barrault. 2017b. Nmtpy: A flexible toolkit for advanced neural machine translation systems. *The Prague Bulletin of Mathematical Linguistics*, 109(1):15–28.

I. Calixto, Q. Liu, and N. Campbell. 2017a. Doubly-attentive decoder for multi-modal neural machine translation. *arXiv:1702.01287*.

I. Calixto, Q. Liu, and N. Campbell. 2017b. Incorporating global visual features into attention-based neural machine translation. *arXiv:1701.06521*.

Q. Cao and D. Xiong. 2018. Encoding gated translation memory into neural machine translation. In *EMNLP*, pages 3042–3047.

J. Chung, C. Gulcehre, K. Cho, and Y. Bengio. 2014. Empirical evaluation of gated recurrent neural networks on sequence modeling. *arXiv:1412.3555*.

J. H. Clark, C. Dyer, A. Lavie, Alon, and N. A. Smith. 2011. Better hypothesis testing for statistical machine translation: Controlling for optimizer instability. In *ACL*, pages 176–181. ACL.

J. Delbrouck and S. Dupont. 2017. An empirical study on the effectiveness of images in multimodal neural machine translation. *arXiv:1707.00995*.

M. Denkowski and A. Lavie. 2014. Meteor universal: Language specific translation evaluation for any target language. In *ICML*, pages 376–380.

D. Dong, H. Wu, W. He, D. Yu, and H. Wang. 2015. Multi-task learning for multiple language translation. In *ACL*, pages 1723–1732.

D. Elliott. 2018. Adversarial evaluation of multimodal machine translation. In *EMNLP*, pages 2974–2978.

D. Elliott, S. Frank, L. Barrault, F. Bougares, and L. Specia. 2017. Findings of the second shared task on multimodal machine translation and multilingual image description. *arXiv:1710.07177*.

D. Elliott, S. Frank, K. Sima'an, and L. Specia. 2016. Multi30k: Multilingual english-german image descriptions. *arXiv:1605.00459*.

O. Firat and K. Cho. 2016. Conditional gated recurrent unit with attention mechanism. *System BLEU baseline*, 31.

O. Firat, K. Cho, and Y. Bengio. 2016. Multi-way, multilingual neural machine translation with a shared attention mechanism. *arXiv:1601.01073*.

E. Garmash and C. Monz. 2016. Ensemble learning for multi-source neural machine translation. In *COLING*, pages 1409–1418.

K. He, X. Zhang, S. Ren, and J. Sun. 2016a. Deep residual learning for image recognition. In *CVPR*, pages 770–778.

K. He, X. Zhang, S. Ren, and J. Sun. 2016b. Identity mappings in deep residual networks. In *ECCV*, pages 630–645. Springer.

J. Helcl, J. Libovický, and D. Varis. 2018. Cuni system for the wmt18 multimodal translation task. In *WMT*, pages 616–623.

J. Hitschler, S. Schamoni, and S. Riezler. 2016. Multimodal pivots for image caption translation. *arXiv:1601.03916*.

P. Huang, F. Liu, S. Shiang, J. Oh, and C. Dyer. 2016. Attention-based multimodal neural machine translation. In *WMT*, pages 639–645.

Julia Ive, Pranava Madhyastha, and Lucia Specia. 2019. Distilling translations with visual awareness. *arXiv preprint arXiv:1906.07701*.

N. Kalchbrenner and P. Blunsom. 2013. Recurrent continuous translation models. In *EMNLP*, pages 1700–1709.

P. Koehn, H. Hoang, A. Birch, C. Callison-Burch, M. Federico, N. Bertoldi, B. Cowan, W. Shen, C. Moran, R. Zens, and et al. 2007. Moses: Open source toolkit for statistical machine translation. In *ACL*, pages 177–180. Association for Computational Linguistics.

Alina Kuznetsova, Hassan Rom, Neil Alldrin, Jasper Uijlings, Ivan Krasin, Jordi Pont-Tuset, Shahab Kamali, Stefan Popov, Matteo Malloci, Tom Duerig, et al. 2018. The open images dataset v4: Unified image classification, object detection, and visual relationship detection at scale. *arXiv preprint arXiv:1811.00982*.

C. Lala, P. S. Madhyastha, C. Scarton, and L. Specia. 2018. Sheffield submissions for wmt18 multimodal translation shared task. In *ICML*, pages 624–631.

J. Libovický and J. Helcl. 2017. Attention strategies for multi-source sequence-to-sequence learning. *arXiv:1704.06567*.

J. Libovický and J. Helcl. 2018. End-to-end non-autoregressive neural machine translation with connectionist temporal classification. *arXiv:1811.04719*.

J. Libovický, J. Helcl, M. Tlustý, P. Pecina, and O. Bojar. 2016. Cuni system for wmt16 automatic post-editing and multimodal translation tasks. *arXiv:1606.07481*.

T. Lin, M. Maire, S. Belongie, J. Hays, P. Perona, D. Ramanan, P. Dollár, and C. L. Zitnick. 2014. Microsoft coco: Common objects in context. In *ECCV*, pages 740–755. Springer.

J. Mao, W. Xu, Y. Yang, J. Wang, and A. L. Yuille. 2014. Explain images with multimodal recurrent neural networks. *arXiv:1410.1090*.

J. Ngiam, A. Khosla, M. Kim, J. Nam, H. Lee, and A. Y. Ng. 2011. Multimodal deep learning. In *ICML*, pages 689–696.

K. Papineni, S. Roukos, T. Ward, and W. Zhu. 2002. Bleu: a method for automatic evaluation of machine translation. In *ACL*, pages 311–318. Association for Computational Linguistics.

S. Ren, K. He, R. Girshick, and J. Sun. 2015. Faster r-cnn: Towards real-time object detection with region proposal networks. In *Advances in neural information processing systems*, pages 91–99.

O. Russakovsky, J. Deng, H. Su, J. Krause, S. Satheesh, S. Ma, Z. Huang, A. Karpathy, A. Khosla, M. Bernstein, and et al. 2015. Imagenet large scale visual recognition challenge. *International Journal of Computer Vision*, 115(3):211–252.

R. Sennrich, B. Haddow, and A. Birch. 2015. Neural machine translation of rare words with subword units. *arXiv:1508.07909*.

M. Snover, B. Dorr, R. Schwartz, L. Micciulla, and J. Makhoul. 2006. A study of translation edit rate with targeted human annotation. In *ICML*, volume 200.

L. Specia, S. Frank, K. Sima'an, and D. Elliott. 2016. A shared task on multimodal machine translation and crosslingual image description. In *ICML*, volume 2, pages 543–553.

I. Sutskever, O. Vinyals, and Q. V. Le. 2014. Sequence to sequence learning with neural networks. In *NIPS*, pages 3104–3112.

O. Vinyals, A. Toshev, S. Bengio, and D. Erhan. 2015. Show and tell: A neural image caption generator. In *CVPR*, pages 3156–3164.

K. Xu, J. Ba, R. Kiros, K. Cho, A. Courville, R. Salakhudinov, R. Zemel, and Y. Bengio. 2015. Show, attend and tell: Neural image caption generation with visual attention. In *ICML*, pages 2048–2057.

P. Young, A. Lai, M. Hodosh, and J. Hockenmaier. 2014. From image descriptions to visual denotations: New similarity metrics for semantic inference over event descriptions. *ACL*, 2:67–78.

Zhuosheng Zhang, Kehai Chen, Rui Wang, Masao Utiyama, Eiichiro Sumita, Zuchao Li, and Hai Zhao. 2019. Neural machine translation with universal visual representation. In *International Conference on Learning Representations*.

R. Zheng, Y. Yang, M. Ma, and L. Huang. 2018. Ensemble sequence level training for multimodal mt: Osu-baidu wmt18 multimodal machine translation system report. *arXiv:1808.10592*.

M. Zhou, R. Cheng, Y. J. Lee, and Z. Yu. 2018. A visual attention grounding neural model for multimodal machine translation. *arXiv:1808.08266*.

B. Zoph and K. Knight. 2016. Multi-source neural translation. *arXiv:1601.00710*.

Error Causal inference for Multi-Fusion models

Chengxi Li
University of Kentucky
Lexington, KY 40506
chengxili@uky.edu

Brent Harrison
University of Kentucky
Lexington, KY 40506
harrison@cs.uky.edu

Abstract

In this paper, we propose an error causal inference method that could be used for finding dominant features for a faulty instance under a well-trained multi-modality input model, which could apply to any testing instance. We evaluate our method using a well-trained multi-modalities stylish caption generation model and find those causal inferences that could provide us the insights for next step optimization.

1 Introduction

As machine learning models become more complex and training data become bigger, it is harder for humans to find errors manually once some output went wrong. This problem is exacerbated by the black box nature of most machine learning models. When a model fails, it can be difficult to determine where the error comes from. This is especially true in problems that are inherently multimodal, such as image captioning, where often multiple models are combined together in order to produce an output. This lack of transparency or ability to perform a vulnerability analysis can be a major hindrance to machine learning practitioners when faced with a model that doesn't perform as expected.

Recently, more and more people begin to fuse text and visual information for downstreaming task. In many cases, these models utilize specialized, pre-trained models to extract features. In these situations, it is highly likely that the source of these errors is from these pre-trained networks either being misused or not being interpreted correctly by the larger machine learning architecture. In this paper, we explore how one would perform a vulnerability analysis in these situations. Specifically, we are interested in identifying model errors likely caused by these pre-trained networks. Specifically, we aim to diagnose these errors by systematically removing elements of the larger machine learning model to pinpoint what the causes of errors happen

to be. This is especially critical in tasks that utilize multi-modality input models since often these models utilize attention. If the model attends to the wrong features, then this error could potentially cascade throughout the network. In other words, we seek to answer the question, "Given a trained model M which has input features x, y, z, if the current test example is not performing well, is that because of the given features or not? If it is, which specific feature is more likely to blame?"

By answering this question, we can give machine learning practitioners, specifically those who are inexperienced with machine learning and AI concepts, some direction in how to improve the performance of their architecture. We summarize our contributions as follows: 1. we provide a practical method to discover causal errors for multi-modality input ML models; 2. we explore how this method can be applied to state-of-the-art machine learning models for performing stylish image captioning; 3. Evaluate our method by through a case study in which we assess whether we can improve the performance of the investigated instance by removing or replacing these problematic features.

2 Related Work

Our approach to sourcing these errors uses causal inference (Peters et al., 2016; Hernán and Robins, 2020). In this section, we will review works related to causal inference as well as works that provided the inspiration for this paper.

Invariance Principle Invariance principle has been used for finding general causal for some outcome under designed treatment process, where people desired to find actual effect of a specific phenomenon. Invariant causal prediction (Peters et al., 2016) has been proposed to offer an practical way to find casuals under linear model assumption. It later got extended to nonlinear model and data (Heinze-Deml et al., 2018). This invariance can be roughly phrased as the outcome Y of some model

11

Proceedings of the Second Workshop on Advances in Language and Vision Research, pages 11–15
©2021 Association for Computational Linguistics

M would not change due to environment change once given the cause for this Y. An example of an *environment change* when $Y = M(X, Z, W)$ and the cause for Y is X, could be a change on Z or W. The invariance principle has been popularly used in machine learning models to train causal models (Arjovsky et al., 2019; Rojas-Carulla et al., 2018). We are going to employ the same insight, using the invariance principle to find cause in our paper but landing in different perspectives. We are not intended to train a model, instead, we are going to use the well-trained models to derive the source cause for lower performance instances.

Potential Outcome and Counterfactual. (Rubin, 2005) proposed using potential outcomes for estimating causal effects. Potential outcomes present the values of the outcome variable Y for each case at a particular point in time after certain actions. But usually, we can only observe one of the potential outcome since situations are based on executing mutually exclusive actions (e.g. give the treatment or don't give the treatment). The unobserved outcome is called the "counterfactual" outcome. In this paper we can observe the counterfactual by removing certain input features from the language generation based on multi-input task.

Debugging Errors Caused by Feature Deficiencies This paper is also related to debugging errors from input. While we are more focus on using a causal inference way to get the real cause for low performance rather than only exploring associations (Amershi et al., 2015; Kang et al., 2018)

3 Methodology

The goal of this paper is to perform a causal analysis in order to determine the likely source of errors in a well-trained model. In the following sections, we will outline our underlying hypotheses related to this task and go into details on the task itself.

3.1 Hypothesis

Hypothesis 1: *With a fixed model, if the output of an instance k is unchanged after an intervention, I, then this is called* **output invariance**. *The causes of the output for this instance k are irrelevant to the features associated the intervention, I.*

Using this output invariance principle, we can identify features that are irrelevant to the prediction made. After removing these irrelevant features, the ones that remain should contribute to any errors present in the output. Given the strictness of the output invariance principle, it is often the case that very few features are identified as the cause of any error present. In some cases, no features are identified. In this paper, we are interested in determining the cause of errors by masking out certain features, specifically those that are unlikely to be the cause of an error. As such, we are interested in the specific case where the removal of certain features does not cause the performance of the model to improve. This phenomenon, which we refer to as **output non-increasing** will be rephrased below.

Hypothesis 2: *With a fixed model, if the output of an instance, k, after an intervention, I, is either less than or equal to the original performance of instance k, then this is called* **output non-increasing**. *Then, the features associated with intervention, I, are likely irrelevant to the cause of any error.*

In this paper, we specifically perform interventions that involving masking/hammering out certain input features. *Hammering out* features could mean zero out input features or specific weights, or even remove certain input modalities, etc.. In this paper we will change the values of certain input features f to 0. Then, output is regenerated according to this new input. If the output is unchanged (or gets worse), then we will remove this feature f from the causal features list. Before we perform these interventions, we first want to identify the errors which do not relate to any of these features. This leads to the next hypothesis.

Hypothesis 3: *If we hammered out all input features and output invariance still holds for instance k, we will record the cause for instance k having lower performance as being due to model and dataset bias. We will refer to this as* **bias error**.

In this paper, we are interested in more than bias errors. With this goal, we arrive at our final hypothesis on performing causal inference for identifying errors.

Hypothesis 4: *If the performance of instance k is poor and the output of instance k is not caused by bias errors, and if all interventions keep feature $f^\star$ unchanged and we still have output non-increasing, we will say $f^\star$ is the error feature which causes the lower performance output for k.*

With all of the above hypotheses we can infer whether the low performance of the instance k is caused by a single feature f or not. Next we will show how these hypotheses can be utilized to identify the causes of errors.

3.2 Causal Graph: with and without Hammering out Features

As we know, when we build a model in deep learning, we always assume a casual graph in advance and then fit data into the graph for training. Figure 1 shows a sample causal graph (a) with multiple input features. These features will be fit into a black box model and finally the model will, in this case, generate some set of output text. Once we have finished training, we will be able to deploy the model and see each testing instance's performance. With a well-trained model, we can perform many interventions, or investigate specific features by intervening on them in different environments. In practice, however, it is impossible for us to obtain all the random environments. Based hypotheses 3 and 4, along with the steps that people take to perform causal predictions in linear (Peters et al., 2016) and non-linear (Heinze-Deml et al., 2018) situations, we, in this paper, give a more detailed and practical definition below to help us identify whether a feature set S is the causal feature set or not when an instance k having error and this error is not a bias error defined in hypothesis 3. Here S could be a feature set composed of a single feature or multiple features. After hamming out some features, we call a remaining feature set P as S's **parental set** when $S \subset P$. We denote $\mathcal{F}_S$ as: $\mathcal{F}_S = \{g(P) \mid P \text{ is a parental set of } S\}$ and

$$g(P) = \begin{cases} P & \text{if } P \text{ satisfies output} \\ & \text{non-increasing,} \\ \emptyset & \text{otherwise.} \end{cases}$$

Then we could extract the estimated causal feature set $\hat{F}$ as:

$$\hat{F} = \bigcap_{F:F\in\mathcal{F}_S} F \tag{1}$$

To simply understand above, we basically check all the parental sets of S on output non-increasing property to finally make decision on whether S is an error casual feature set or not. In this paper, we mainly focus on evaluating single feature set. To better explain, we also display all the interventions (b-h in Figure 1) we have done to the features (masking out some features) when there are a total of 3 features in the assumed causal graph. We will infer the causal feature for a low performance instance k based on all of these potential outcomes before and after interventions. We will use $o_x, x \in \{a, b, c...h\}$ to note the score for output

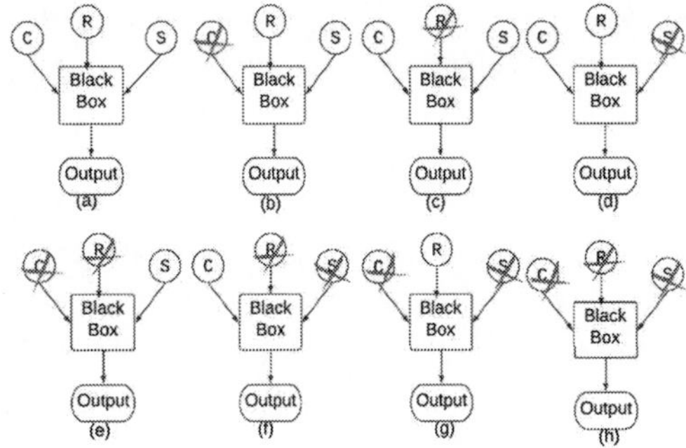

Figure 1: Displays the causal graph with various sets of features zeroed out and a red cross mark signifies zeroing out

generation of graphs in Figure 1. First, we extract the instances when the error cause is independent of any features where we find all the instances $\mathcal{B}$, which satisfy $o_a == o_h$. Then the following causal feature inferences will exclude detected instances in $\mathcal{B}$ first. As we are specifically interested in single feature errors, we will enumerate the situation when causal features are R, C, S for instance k, respectively. First of all, according to hypothesis 3 and 4, k $\notin \mathcal{B}$. The causal feature is S when: $o_a >= o_b >= o_c >= o_e$; The causal feature is C when: $o_a >= o_c >= o_d >= o_f$; The causal feature is R when: $o_a >= o_b >= o_d >= o_g$.

It is important to note that removing an error feature does not necessarily mean that the performance will increase, as it is possible that there are other sources of errors that still keep performance low. In these rules, we use the "=" sign in its strictest sense. However, one can always use it in a way that is interchangeable with "very similar." For example, if the difference between two output scores is 10^{-16}, you can choose to regard these two scores as equal per your needs.

4 Experiment

To show the effectiveness of our approach, we will examine its performance on a stylish image captioning task that uses multi-modality feature fusion. While we focus on this task as an example, this approach could be applied to many other domains.

4.1 Dataset

We have chosen the dataset and the task based on three qualities:the work has a well-trained saved model which we could use for intervention and inference; this work still has room to be improved by identifying and removing the source of potential errors; the work utilizes multiple input features in a way that enables removing said features.

Specifically, we choose the work on the 3M model (Li and Harrison, 2021) for stylish text captioning. We do this because it relies on generating captions using several input features including pre-trained text features (C), ResNext features (R), and style information (S) as an input. We would like to explore whether these input features have caused problems when instances are under performing. The dataset we examine is the test set from the PERSONALITY-CAPTIONS dataset (Shuster et al., 2019) using in Li and Harrison's work along with the pretrained model they provide [1]. Even though we use its test set in our experiment, our method could be applied on any set of data of any size when there is a debugging need for multi-fusion models. We will leave this for future work.

4.2 Implementing details

Specifically, we define an instance is under performance in 3M (Li and Harrison, 2021) when the BLEU1 (Papineni et al., 2002) score is lower than the median BLEU1 value among all testing data. In total, we have investigated 9981 instances and 4982 of them are classified as under performing. 74 of these have been detected as bias errors. So finally, 4908 instances have been examined for single feature errors.

We first perform causal inference for style feature and denote those instances that have style error as K_s. Then perform the causal finding steps for ResNext and dense captions without differentiating the order in the remaining instances. The reason to decide such order is due to the structure of 3M, where style is used globally to refine ResNext and dense captions for later stylish text generations while ResNext and dense caption have the same importance for text generations.

4.3 Evaluation

The reason to find the cause for the errors is that we would like to further improve a model when it is well-trained or make a remedy when the model is malfunctioned, especially from the source side. Thus, we evaluate casual predictions by evaluating whether we could improve the model's performance by just altering the causal feature. There are many potential treatments that we could make on the source side such as data augmentation, feature replacement, or feature removal. For each instance k with predicted causal feature f, if its performance could be improved by improving f, then we will judge the causal error inference for this instance k as correct, otherwise incorrect. More details on the specific interventions we use are outlined below: Style: (S1) replace current style with 5 other well-trained styles S, where most instances with style s, $s \in S$ has better BLEU1 score than the medium BLEU1 score. (S2) remove Style. Dense Caption: (C1) replace dense caption to ground truth; (C2) remove dense caption. Resnext: (R1) replace dense caption to ground truth and then remove Resnext, where we make sure at least one of the visual features is valid. (R2) remove Resnext.

We will record the best output BLEU1 score after each intervention. If the intervention results in a higher BLEU1 score than the output prior to the intervention, then the feature in question will be marked as the cause of an error. For all the instances which have been ascribed by a feature f, we calculate the percentage of those in which the BLEU1 score could be improved and report them in Table 1.

5 Result and Discussion

The result is shown in the Table 1. We see that for each feature, most of the instances have increased their performance by improving the predicted features. This performance is also a conservative value as we only did limited feature improvements. For example, for Resnext, we have no better features available and, thus, could not do a replacement. Also in Table 1, the style feature is the most predicted error causal feature among all three feature modalities. We have 1041 instances point its performance error towards style. We speculate this is resulting from the weak training of a certain set of styles, since the BLEU score can be improved if replaced with other better-trained styles for 89.4% of these instances. To further investigate this, we report the frequency of the styles in those 1041 instances in Figure 2 and intend to see whether the estimated error styles are distributed sparsely (all styles are not trained well) or densely (a certain set of styles is not trained well). From Figure 2 we can see that many styles repeatedly appear as errors for various instances, which aligns our speculation. With these predicted error styles, we can either do

Table 1: The evaluation result for each feature under casual inference. Predictions Count are the number of instances predicted with corresponding feature errors.

Feature	Predictions Count	Improvement(%)
Style	1041	0.894
Dense Caption	378	0.797
Resnext	300	0.769

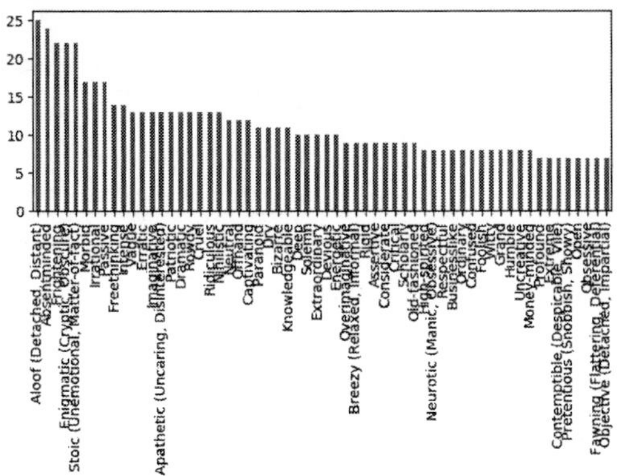

Figure 2: The styles are those frequently predicted as the causal errors; the horizontal bar represents the frequency. Here we select the top 50 styles.

some data augmentation to cover the gap between training and testing or redesign the training process to enable the model to focus more intently on these styles.

6 Conclusion

In this paper, we apply an extended invariance principle to provide a method for performing error causal inference. We evaluate our method under on a stylish image captioning model that uses multimodal fusion in its input features. We show that we could improve the performance of this model based on simply removing or replacing those found causal errors. Over 70% of the predicted errors could be modified to improve performance. Also, our method is model-agnostic, it could be used for different fusion model for optimization, debugging or assessing purpose.

References

Saleema Amershi, Max Chickering, Steven M Drucker, Bongshin Lee, Patrice Simard, and Jina Suh. 2015. Modeltracker: Redesigning performance analysis tools for machine learning. In *Proceedings of the 33rd Annual ACM Conference on Human Factors in Computing Systems*, pages 337–346.

Martin Arjovsky, Léon Bottou, Ishaan Gulrajani, and David Lopez-Paz. 2019. Invariant risk minimization. *arXiv preprint arXiv:1907.02893*.

Christina Heinze-Deml, Jonas Peters, and Nicolai Meinshausen. 2018. Invariant causal prediction for nonlinear models. *Journal of Causal Inference*, 6(2).

Miguel A Hernán and James M Robins. 2020. Causal inference: what if.

Daniel Kang, Deepti Raghavan, Peter Bailis, and Matei Zaharia. 2018. Model assertions for debugging machine learning. In *NeurIPS MLSys Workshop*.

Chengxi Li and Brent Harrison. 2021. 3m: Multi-style image caption generation using multi-modality features under multi-updown model.

Kishore Papineni, Salim Roukos, Todd Ward, and Wei-Jing Zhu. 2002. Bleu: a method for automatic evaluation of machine translation. In *Proceedings of the 40th annual meeting on association for computational linguistics*, pages 311–318. Association for Computational Linguistics.

Jonas Peters, Peter Bühlmann, and Nicolai Meinshausen. 2016. Causal inference by using invariant prediction: identification and confidence intervals. *Journal of the Royal Statistical Society. Series B (Statistical Methodology)*, pages 947–1012.

Mateo Rojas-Carulla, Bernhard Schölkopf, Richard Turner, and Jonas Peters. 2018. Invariant models for causal transfer learning. *The Journal of Machine Learning Research*, 19(1):1309–1342.

Donald B Rubin. 2005. Causal inference using potential outcomes: Design, modeling, decisions. *Journal of the American Statistical Association*, 100(469):322–331.

Kurt Shuster, Samuel Humeau, Hexiang Hu, Antoine Bordes, and Jason Weston. 2019. Engaging image captioning via personality. In *Proceedings of the IEEE/CVF Conference on Computer Vision and Pattern Recognition*, pages 12516–12526.

Leveraging Partial Dependency Trees to Control Image Captions

Wenjie Zhong
The University of Tokyo
zvengin@is.s.u-tokyo.ac.jp

Yusuke Miyao
The University of Tokyo
yusuke@is.s.u-tokyo.ac.jp

Abstract

Controlling the generation of image captions attracts lots of attention recently. In this paper, we propose a framework leveraging *partial syntactic dependency trees* as control signals to make image captions include specified words and their syntactic structures. To achieve this purpose, we propose a *Syntactic Dependency Structure Aware Model* (**SDSAM**), which explicitly learns to generate the syntactic structures of image captions to include given partial dependency trees. In addition, we come up with a metric to evaluate how many specified words and their syntactic dependencies are included in generated captions. We carry out experiments on two standard datasets: Microsoft COCO and Flickr30k. Empirical results show that image captions generated by our model are effectively controlled in terms of specified words and their syntactic structures. The code is available on GitHub[1].

1 Introduction

Controllable image captioning emerges as a popular research topic in recent years. Existing works attempt to enhance models' controllability and captions' diversity by controlling the attributes of image captions such as style (Mathews et al., 2016), sentiments (Gan et al., 2017), contents (Dai et al., 2018; Cornia et al., 2019; Zhong et al., 2020) and part-of-speech (Deshpande et al., 2019). However, some important attributes of image captions like words and syntactic structures, are ignored in previous works. For example, for the image in the Figure 2, the work (Cornia et al., 2019) specifies a set of objects like 'dog, man, frisebee' as a control signal, but there still exist lots of possibilities of composing them into different captions, such as 'a dog and a man play frisebee on grass' and 'a dog playing with a man catches frisebee', since both words and syntactic structures are not determined yet.

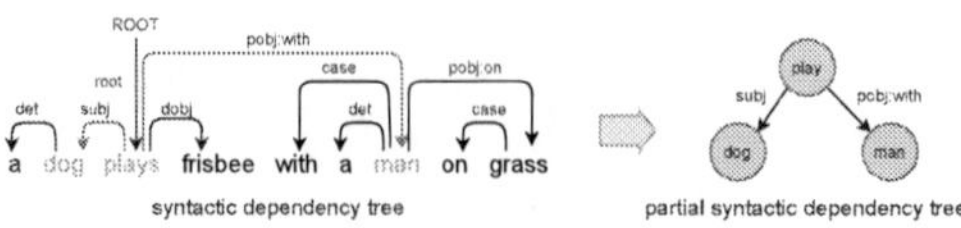

Figure 1: An example of syntactic dependency tree(left) and partial dependency tree (right)

To address this challenging issue, we propose a framework, which employs *partial dependency trees* as control signals. As shown in Figure 1, a partial dependency tree, a sub-tree of a syntactic dependency tree, contains words and their syntactic structures, and thus we can utilize it to specify control information about words and their syntactic structures.

In addition, we develop a pipeline model called *syntactic dependency structure-aware model* (SD-SAM) which first derives a full syntactic dependency tree and then flatten it into a caption. The motivation behind this pipeline model is that we assume explicitly generating syntactic dependency trees as intermediate representations can better help the model learn how to apply the specified syntactic information to the captions and the intermediate representations can give users an intuitive impression on which part of the captions' syntactic structures is controlled.

Finally, we propose a syntactic dependency-based evaluation metric which evaluates whether the generated captions have been controlled in terms of syntactic structures. Our metric is computed based on the overlap of syntactic dependencies which is different from existing metrics like BLEU (Papineni et al., 2002), METEOR (Denkowski and Lavie, 2014), ROUGE (Lin, 2004), CIDEr (Vedantam et al., 2015) and SPICE (Anderson et al., 2018) which rely on the overlap of n-grams or semantic graphs. Empirical results show that image captions generated by our model are effectively controlled in terms of specified words and their syntactic structures.

Proceedings of the Second Workshop on Advances in Language and Vision Research, pages 16–21
©2021 Association for Computational Linguistics

---

[1]https://github.com/ZVengin/DepControl_ALVR

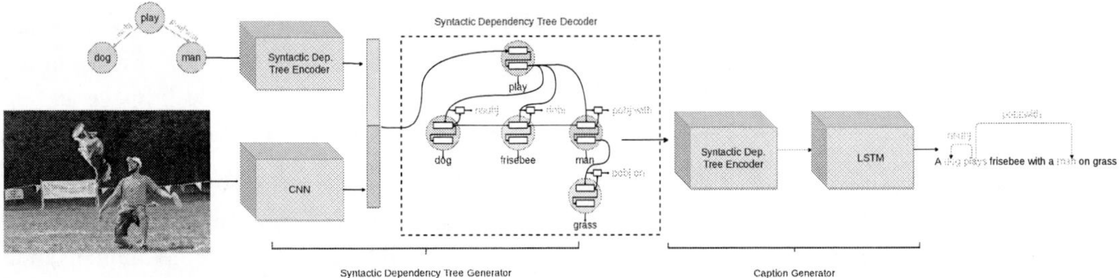

Figure 2: Model architecture: our model generates captions in two steps: (1) generating syntactic dependency tree using syntactic dependency tree generator. (2) flatting it into a caption using caption generator.

2 Framework Definition

The task presented in this paper is defined as generating a caption sentence (i.e. word sequence) $y = \langle w_1, \cdots, w_{|y|} \rangle$ given an image I and a partial dependency tree P as input, so that the dependency tree T_y of y includes P as far as possible. The syntactic dependency tree of a sentence, as shown in Figure 1, refers to a tree structure to represent syntactic relations between words. A syntactic dependency tree T_x of a sentence $x = \langle w_1, \cdots, w_{|x|} \rangle$ is defined as a set of dependencies, $\{D_1, D_2, \cdots, D_{|T_x|}\}$, where $|T_x|$ denotes the number of dependencies in T_x. Each dependency D_k is expressed in the form of $w_i \xrightarrow{e_{i,j}} w_j$, where w_i and w_j are the head word and the dependent word of D_k, and $e_{i,j}$ is the dependency label. We denote child nodes of w_i as $C(w_i)$; i.e. $C(w_i) = \{w_j | w_i \xrightarrow{e_{i,j}} w_j \in T_x\}$. A partial dependency tree P here refers to a sub-tree of the syntactic dependency tree of some sentence. That is, $P \subseteq T_x$ for some sentence x.

3 Syntactic Dependency Structure Aware Model

The syntactic dependency structure-aware model(SDSAM) shown in Figure 2 generates image captions in two steps: (1) the syntactic dependency tree generator on the left part derives a full syntactic dependency tree from the image and the partial dependency tree. (2) the caption generator on the right part will flatten the syntactic dependency tree into a caption.

The Syntactic Dependency Tree Generator
The syntactic dependency tree generator encodes the input image with a CNN network implemented with Resent152 (He et al., 2016) into image features and encodes the partial dependency tree with a syntactic dependency tree encoder implemented with Tree-LSTM (Tai et al., 2015) into partial dependency tree features.

After combining the image features and the partial dependency tree features, the syntactic dependency tree generator derives the full syntactic dependency tree using the syntactic dependency tree decoder from the combined features s. The syntactic dependency tree decoder consists of two attention modules, Attn_{in} and Attn_{out}, and two interweaved GRU networks (Cho et al., 2014), GRU_v and GRU_h. The decoding process is carried out from the root node to leaf nodes in a top-down manner. For a node w_i, its child nodes are decoded one by one from left-to-right. Each child node is predicted based on the information of its parent node and its left sibling node generated in previous steps. At the mean while, the attention modules highlight the words to be generated for the current child node. Assuming we decode the child w_j of node w_i, the hidden state of node w_i and node w_j are denoted as h_i and h_j respectively. The left sibling of node w_j is denoted as w_{j-1} and its hidden state as h_{j-1}. For each input image, we detect a set of keywords $c = \{r_1, \cdots, r_{|c|}\}$ following the method proposed in (You et al., 2016), and encode c into a matrix $C \in \mathbb{R}^{E_w \times |c|}$, where E_w is the size of word embedding.

$$h_0 = U^{(s)} s \tag{1}$$

$$\tilde{h}_i = \text{GRU}_v(h_i, w_i) \tag{2}$$

$$c_{\text{in}} = \text{Attn}_{\text{in}}(w_i, C) \tag{3}$$

$$h_j = \text{GRU}_h(\tilde{h}_i, [h_{j-1}; w_{j-1}; c_{\text{in}}]) \tag{4}$$

$$c_{\text{out}} = \text{Attn}_{\text{out}}(h_j, C) \tag{5}$$

$$w_j \sim \text{Softmax}(U^{(w)} h_j + V^{(w)} c_{\text{out}}) \tag{6}$$

$$e_{i,j} \sim \text{Softmax}(U^{(e)} h_j + V^{(e)} \tilde{h}_i) \tag{7}$$

17

where:

$$\text{Attn}(\boldsymbol{q}, \boldsymbol{C}) = \boldsymbol{C}\boldsymbol{\alpha} \tag{8}$$

$$\boldsymbol{\alpha} = \text{Softmax}(\boldsymbol{A}^{\mathsf{T}}\boldsymbol{v}) \tag{9}$$

$$\boldsymbol{A} = \tanh(\boldsymbol{U}^{(\alpha)}(\boldsymbol{q} \cdot \boldsymbol{1}^{\mathsf{T}}) + \boldsymbol{V}^{(\alpha)}\boldsymbol{C}) \tag{10}$$

In the above formulas, $\boldsymbol{U}^{(s)} \in \mathbb{R}^{H \times E_s}$, $\boldsymbol{U}^{(w)} \in \mathbb{R}^{V_w \times H}$, $\boldsymbol{U}^{(e)} \in \mathbb{R}^{V_e \times H}$, $\boldsymbol{U}^{(\alpha)} \in \mathbb{R}^{E_a \times E_q}$, $\boldsymbol{V}^{(w)} \in \mathbb{R}^{V_w \times H}$, $\boldsymbol{V}^{(e)} \in \mathbb{R}^{V_e \times H}$ and $\boldsymbol{V}^{(\alpha)} \in \mathbb{R}^{E_a \times E_w}$ are parameters for reshaping features. Here E_s, E_a and E_q are the size of the input feature s, the attention feature $\boldsymbol{A}$ and the query $\boldsymbol{q}$ respectively. V_w and V_e are the vocabulary size for the node and edge respectively and H is the size of hidden states. In equation (10), $\boldsymbol{v} \in \mathbb{R}^{E_a \times 1}$ is a parameter and $\boldsymbol{1} \in \mathbb{R}^{|c| \times 1}$ is a vector with all elements being one.

The Caption Generator The caption generator takes the syntactic dependency tree generated in the first step as input and encodes it with the syntactic dependency tree encoder into syntactic dependency tree features. The caption generator combines it with image features extracted in the first step and use the combined features to initialize the LSTM decoder (Hochreiter and Schmidhuber, 1997) to generate the caption.

4 Experiment

Preparing Datasets with Partial Dependency Trees For evaluation, we apply two methods to create partial dependency trees for on Microsoft COCO (Chen et al., 2015) and Flickr30k (Young et al., 2014). The first method extracts partial dependency trees from reference captions. We parsing reference captions to syntactic dependency trees using Spacy [2] and then randomly sample subsets from each syntactic dependency tree. Sampled partial dependency trees are then paired with corresponding reference captions. The dataset created by this procedure is denoted as $test_{gold}$ in Section 5.

The other method creates partial dependency trees from images in two steps: (1) we first train a syntactic dependency classifier to predict syntactic dependencies for an input image. (2) Predicted syntactic dependencies are combined to form a syntactic dependency graph for the input image, from which partial dependency trees are sampled. The dataset created by this procedure is denoted as $test_{pred}$ in Section 5.

For training, following the first method, we directly sample a partial dependency tree from one of the reference captions for each image and the paired reference caption is used as a training target.

Evaluation Metric The evaluation metrics for image captioning fall into two categories: (1)Quality: evaluating the relevance to human annotations with metrics including BLEU (Papineni et al., 2002) and METEOR (Denkowski and Lavie, 2014); ROUGE (Lin, 2004), and CIDEr (Vedantam et al., 2015) and SPICE (Anderson et al., 2018). (2)Control-ability: evaluating whether generated image captions are successfully controlled by partial dependency trees. We devise a new metric called *Dependency Based Evaluation Metric* (**DBEM**) for this purpose. Assuming that a partial dependency tree $P = \{D_1, \cdots, D_{|P|}\}$ is input, DBEM calculates how many syntactic dependencies specified in the partial dependency tree are included in the dependency tree T_y of generated caption y. The DBEM score for the evaluation dataset is given as an average of this score for each input. Formally,

$$DBEM(P, T_y) = \frac{\sum_{D \in P} \mathbf{1}(D, T_y)}{|P|}, \tag{11}$$

$$\mathbf{1}(D, T) = \begin{cases} 1 & \text{if } D \in T \\ 0 & \text{if } D \notin T. \end{cases} \tag{12}$$

Experiment Setting The training of our model is split into two stages including training the syntactic dependency tree generator and training the caption generator. We set the size of hidden states to be 512, the word embedding size to be 512, and the dependency label embedding size to be 300. We train our model using the Adam optimizer (Kingma and Ba, 2015) with a learning rate $5e^{-4}$ for the first stage and $1e^{-4}$ for the second stage. Two models, including our SDSAM model and the NIC model (Vinyals et al., 2015) with its encoder being replaced with Resnet152, are compared under three different control inputs. (1) *None* control: input is an image. (2) *Half* control: input is an image and the words of a partial dependency tree. (3) *Full* control: input is an image and a partial dependency tree.

5 Results and Analysis

Quality (1) Results on $test_{gold}$: We show BLEU-4 (B4), METEOR (M), ROUGE (R), CIDEr (C), and SPICE (S) scores on $test_{gold}$ in Table 1, whose

---

[2] https://spacy.io

		Microsoft COCO					Flickr30k				
Control	Model	B-4	M	R	C	S	B-4	M	R	C	S
None	NIC	9.3	15.5	35.6	88.5	21.7	5.9	11.4	28.6	36.3	14.1
	SDSAM	9.6	16.0	35.5	94.4	23.7	4.6	10.8	25.8	34.9	14.8
Half	NIC	25.5	27.3	52.2	232.2	41.9	12.7	18.3	38.3	88.7	26.4
	SDSAM	24.7	26.6	52.6	234.4	44.1	12.4	18.4	40.2	103.8	32.8
Full	NIC	32.5	29.9	58.3	294.1	47.1	15.0	19.1	41.0	105.5	27.7
	SDSAM	30.2	29.2	57.1	282.3	48.4	13.4	18.9	41.5	114.2	33.7

Table 1: Evaluation of quality on $test_{gold}$. Each generated caption is only evaluated against its corresponding reference caption.

		Microsoft COCO					Flickr30k				
Control	Model	B-4	M	R	C	S	B-4	M	R	C	S
None	NIC	27.2	23.8	51.2	86.7	17.1	18.1	18.1	42.8	35.3	11.5
	SDSAM	28.0	24.5	50.9	90.2	18.0	15.8	17.5	39.7	35.6	11.7
Half	NIC	27.9	24.4	52.0	88.4	18.3	18.2	17.6	42.3	32.1	11.9
	SDSAM	26.8	24.4	51.1	88.7	18.5	17.2	17.4	40.5	32.9	12.3
Full	NIC	25.6	24.6	51.0	86.5	18.6	15.7	18.4	41.5	31.2	12.5
	SDSAM	26.0	24.5	50.8	87.7	19.0	16.7	17.7	40.7	32.4	12.4

Table 2: Evaluation of quality on $test_{pred}$. Each generated caption is evaluated against all reference captions of its corresponding image.

partial dependency trees are sampled from reference captions. This table shows that both NIC and SDSAM achieve significant improvements on evaluation scores when more control signals are input. This indicates that generated captions become closer to reference captions. These improvements are expectable since control signals contain information of reference captions. This result attests that partial dependency trees carry information useful for generating specific sentences. When both models are given the same control signals, SDSAM has comparable performance to NIC in n-gram based metrics (i.e. BLEU-4, METEOR, ROUGE and CIDEr), while achieving a significantly better performance on SPICE, which is a semantic relation based metric. This result reveals an interesting phenomenon that explicitly learning the syntactic structures of captions can improve performance on the semantic relation based metric.

(2) Results on $test_{pred}$: We show the evaluation results on $test_{pred}$ in Table 2, whose partial dependency trees are generated from images. For NIC and SDSAM, evaluation scores mostly remain the same level, but slight improvements are observed in SPICE. This result reveals that partial dependency trees generated from images do not have a significant impact on the quality of image captions, while giving partial dependency trees as control signals do not harm caption quality. For the same control signals, SDSAM has a better performance

on SPICE in most cases, which follows the results on $test_{gold}$.

Controllability DBEM scores on $test_{gold}$ and $test_{pred}$ are shown in Table 3. The table shows that the DBEM scores of both models are very low when no control is given. This reveals that only a small proportion of syntactic dependencies in partial dependency trees appear in reference captions by chance, indicating that additional input to control syntactic structures is meaningful. When the models are given words as control signals, the DBEM scores are significantly increased, meaning that both models can infer syntactic structures from words even without explicit syntactic structure information. However, it is also clear that nearly half of the specified dependencies are missing in generated captions. These observations suggest that words provide useful information as control signals, but are insufficient to specify syntactic structures completely. When partial dependency trees are input, the DBEM scores further improve significantly. It means that most syntactic dependencies specified in partial dependency trees are included in generated captions. This result demonstrates that syntactic structure information plays an important role in precisely controlling image captions.

When the models are given no control signals, SDSAM has better DBEM scores than NIC. This is possibly because SDSAM explicitly learns to generate syntactic dependency trees, and can bet-

Control	Model	test$_{gold}$		test$_{pred}$	
		MSCOCO	Flickr30k	MSCOCO	Flickr30k
None	NIC	7.1	4.5	12.2	15.5
	SDSAM	9.5	5.4	19.6	19.8
Half	NIC	47.8	33.9	61.4	64.7
	SDSAM	51.4	44.6	64.2	72.3
Full	NIC	68.3	42.7	86.2	85.0
	SDSAM	69.5	52.9	87.1	87.5

Table 3: Evaluation of controllability (DBEM scores)

ter generate high-frequency syntactic dependencies that also frequently appear in partial dependency trees. When the models are given words and/or syntactic dependencies as control signals, SDSAM achieves higher DBEM scores than NIC. This result demonstrates that explicitly learning to generate syntactic dependency trees as an intermediate representation contributes to better controlling of image captions.

6 Case Study

In Figure 3, we show an example of the output from our model on *test$_{pred}$*. Our syntactic dependency classifier first predicts a syntactic dependency graph from the input image. Once the syntactic dependency graph is constructed, we sample three partial dependency trees with different node numbers as shown in the figure. Finally, our SDSAM model infers the captions from the input image and the partial dependency trees. From this example, it is obvious that all words and syntactic structures specified in partial dependency trees also appear in the generated captions. Furthermore, the three generated captions are considerably different from each other, demonstrating that giving partial dependency trees as control signals can improve captions' diversity.

7 Conclusion

We presented a framework for controlling image captions in terms of words and syntactic structures by giving partial dependency trees as control signals. We develop a syntactic dependency structure aware model to explicitly learn the syntactic structures in control signals. Empirical results show that image captions generated by our model are effectively controlled in terms of specified words and their syntactic structures. Furthermore, the results indicate that explicitly learning to generate the syntactic dependency trees of captions enhances the model's controllability.

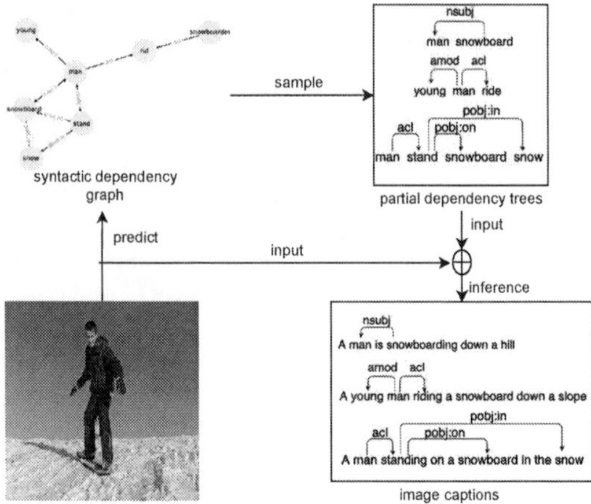

Figure 3: Case study: This figure shows an example generated during inference phase.

References

Peter Anderson, Xiaodong He, Chris Buehler, Damien Teney, Mark Johnson, Stephen Gould, and Lei Zhang. 2018. Bottom-up and top-down attention for image captioning and visual question answering. In *2018 IEEE Conference on Computer Vision and Pattern Recognition, CVPR 2018, Salt Lake City, UT, USA, June 18-22, 2018*, pages 6077–6086. IEEE Computer Society.

Xinlei Chen, Hao Fang, Tsung-Yi Lin, Ramakrishna Vedantam, Saurabh Gupta, Piotr Dollár, and C. Lawrence Zitnick. 2015. Microsoft COCO captions: Data collection and evaluation server. *CoRR*, abs/1504.00325.

Kyunghyun Cho, Bart van Merrienboer, Çaglar Gülçehre, Dzmitry Bahdanau, Fethi Bougares, Holger Schwenk, and Yoshua Bengio. 2014. Learning phrase representations using RNN encoder-decoder for statistical machine translation. In *Proceedings of the 2014 Conference on Empirical Methods in Natural Language Processing, EMNLP 2014, October 25-29, 2014, Doha, Qatar*, pages 1724–1734. Association for Computational Linguistics.

Marcella Cornia, Lorenzo Baraldi, and Rita Cucchiara. 2019. Show, control and tell: A framework for generating controllable and grounded captions. In *IEEE Conference on Computer Vision and Pattern Recognition, CVPR 2019, Long Beach, CA, USA, June 16-20, 2019*, pages 8307–8316. IEEE Computer Society.

Bo Dai, Sanja Fidler, and Dahua Lin. 2018. A neural compositional paradigm for image captioning. In *Advances in Neural Information Processing Systems 31: Annual Conference on Neural Information Processing Systems 2018, NeurIPS 2018, December 3-8, 2018, Montréal, Canada*, pages 656–666.

Michael J. Denkowski and Alon Lavie. 2014. Meteor universal: Language specific translation evaluation for any target language. In *Proceedings of the Ninth Workshop on Statistical Machine Translation, WMT@ACL 2014, June 26-27, 2014, Baltimore, Maryland, USA*, pages 376–380. The Association for Computer Linguistics.

Aditya Deshpande, Jyoti Aneja, Liwei Wang, Alexander G. Schwing, and David A. Forsyth. 2019. Fast, diverse and accurate image captioning guided by part-of-speech. In *IEEE Conference on Computer Vision and Pattern Recognition, CVPR 2019, Long Beach, CA, USA, June 16-20, 2019*, pages 10695–10704. IEEE Computer Society.

Chuang Gan, Zhe Gan, Xiaodong He, Jianfeng Gao, and Li Deng. 2017. Stylenet: Generating attractive visual captions with styles. In *2017 IEEE Conference on Computer Vision and Pattern Recognition, CVPR 2017, Honolulu, HI, USA, July 21-26, 2017*, pages 955–964. IEEE Computer Society.

Kaiming He, Xiangyu Zhang, Shaoqing Ren, and Jian Sun. 2016. Deep residual learning for image recognition. In *2016 IEEE Conference on Computer Vision and Pattern Recognition, CVPR 2016, Las Vegas, NV, USA, June 27-30, 2016*, pages 770–778. IEEE Computer Society.

Sepp Hochreiter and Jürgen Schmidhuber. 1997. Long short-term memory. *Neural Computation*, 9(8):1735–1780.

Diederik P. Kingma and Jimmy Ba. 2015. Adam: A method for stochastic optimization. In *3rd International Conference on Learning Representations, ICLR 2015, San Diego, CA, USA, May 7-9, 2015, Conference Track Proceedings*.

Chin-Yew Lin. 2004. ROUGE: A package for automatic evaluation of summaries. In *Text Summarization Branches Out*, pages 74–81, Barcelona, Spain. Association for Computational Linguistics.

Alexander Patrick Mathews, Lexing Xie, and Xuming He. 2016. Senticap: Generating image descriptions with sentiments. In *Proceedings of the Thirtieth AAAI Conference on Artificial Intelligence, February 12-17, 2016, Phoenix, Arizona, USA*, pages 3574–3580. AAAI Press.

Kishore Papineni, Salim Roukos, Todd Ward, and Wei-Jing Zhu. 2002. Bleu: a method for automatic evaluation of machine translation. In *Proceedings of the 40th Annual Meeting of the Association for Computational Linguistics, July 6-12, 2002, Philadelphia, PA, USA*, pages 311–318. Association for Computational Linguistics.

Kai Sheng Tai, Richard Socher, and Christopher D. Manning. 2015. Improved semantic representations from tree-structured long short-term memory networks. In *Proceedings of the 53rd Annual Meeting of the Association for Computational Linguistics and the 7th International Joint Conference on Natural Language Processing of the Asian Federation of Natural Language Processing, ACL 2015, July 26-31, 2015, Beijing, China, Volume 1: Long Papers*, pages 1556–1566. The Association for Computer Linguistics.

Ramakrishna Vedantam, C. Lawrence Zitnick, and Devi Parikh. 2015. Cider: Consensus-based image description evaluation. In *IEEE Conference on Computer Vision and Pattern Recognition, CVPR 2015, Boston, MA, USA, June 7-12, 2015*, pages 4566–4575. IEEE Computer Society.

Oriol Vinyals, Alexander Toshev, Samy Bengio, and Dumitru Erhan. 2015. Show and tell: A neural image caption generator. In *IEEE Conference on Computer Vision and Pattern Recognition, CVPR 2015, Boston, MA, USA, June 7-12, 2015*, pages 3156–3164. IEEE Computer Society.

Quanzeng You, Hailin Jin, Zhaowen Wang, Chen Fang, and Jiebo Luo. 2016. Image captioning with semantic attention. In *2016 IEEE Conference on Computer Vision and Pattern Recognition, CVPR 2016, Las Vegas, NV, USA, June 27-30, 2016*, pages 4651–4659. IEEE Computer Society.

Peter Young, Alice Lai, Micah Hodosh, and Julia Hockenmaier. 2014. From image descriptions to visual denotations: New similarity metrics for semantic inference over event descriptions. *Trans. Assoc. Comput. Linguistics*, 2:67–78.

Yiwu Zhong, Liwei Wang, Jianshu Chen, Dong Yu, and Yin Li. 2020. Comprehensive image captioning via scene graph decomposition. In *Computer Vision - ECCV 2020 - 16th European Conference, Glasgow, UK, August 23-28, 2020, Proceedings, Part XIV*, volume 12359 of *Lecture Notes in Computer Science*, pages 211–229. Springer.

Grounding Plural Phrases:
Countering Evaluation Biases by Individuation

Julia Suter   **Letitia Parcalabescu**   **Anette Frank**

Department of Computational Linguistics
Heidelberg University, 69120 Heidelberg
`{suter,parcalabescu,frank}@cl.uni-heidelberg.de`

Abstract

Phrase grounding (PG) is a multimodal task that grounds language in images. PG systems are evaluated on well-known benchmarks, using *Intersection over Union (IoU)* as evaluation metric. This work highlights a disconcerting bias in the evaluation of grounded *plural phrases*, which arises from representing *sets of objects* as a *union box* covering all component bounding boxes, in conjunction with the IoU metric. We detect, analyze and quantify an *evaluation bias* in the grounding of plural phrases and define a *novel metric, c-IoU,* based on a union box's component boxes. We experimentally show that our new metric greatly alleviates this bias and recommend using it for fairer evaluation of plural phrases in PG tasks.

1   Introduction

Phrase grounding (PG) describes the multimodal task of identifying objects in images and connecting them to free-form phrases in a textual description (caption). A phrase usually describes one, or sometimes several, specific objects.

Grounding phrases in image regions provides an essential link between texts and images and serves as a foundation for multimodal understanding tasks, including sentence-to-image alignment, Visual QA, Visual Common-sense Reasoning (VCR), etc.

Benchmarks for training and evaluating PG systems (Everingham et al., 2010; Lin et al., 2014; Kazemzadeh et al., 2014; Plummer et al., 2015; Krishna et al., 2017) generally provide rectangular bounding boxes as ground truth (GT). Therefore a PG ground truth is represented as a phrase linking to a (gold) bounding box enclosing the image patch referred to by the phrase. Some datasets provide pixel segmentation masks (Lin et al., 2014), which enable more precise evaluations but are more difficult and costly to produce. Thus, the trend towards annotating bounding boxes persists in recent datasets (Ilinykh et al., 2019).

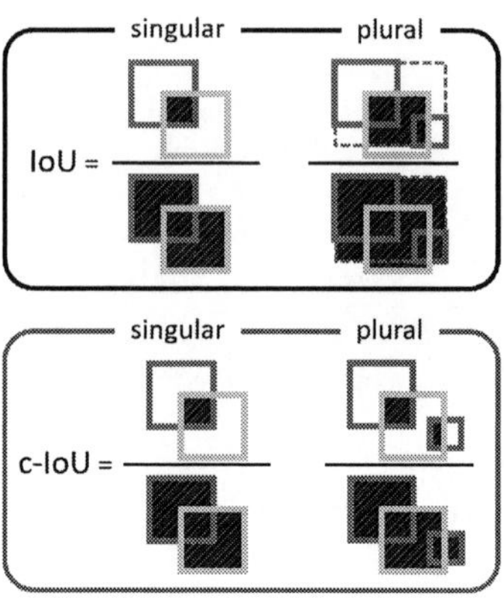

Figure 1: Illustration of how to compute the evaluation metric *IoU* and its adaptation *c-IoU* (with ground truth (GT) bounding boxes in blue, and predicted boxes in yellow). The numerator represents the computed intersection area, the denominator represents the union area. *IoU* and *c-IoU* only differ for plural phrases: *IoU* computes a union box (dashed) covering all components, while *c-IoU only considers* the area of the individual components to compute the intersection and union.

Plural phrases describe multiple entities in an image, either through a collective term (e.g. *crowd*) or a plural form (e.g. *two children*). Depending on the annotation, the gold box consists either of a single box enclosing all entities or several component boxes representing the individual entities. By convention[1], component boxes are merged into one *union box* spanning all individual boxes, functioning as a single gold box. Figure (2.a) gives an example of a union box for a plural phrase with two components. This reduction of multiple boxes to a single union box is widely established in PG evaluation, both for ground truths and predictions.

Although plural phrases are underrepresented in PG benchmarks, they constitute substantial proportions, and appropriate annotation and evaluation of component boxes is essential to achieve high-

---

[1]as, e.g., adopted in Plummer et al. (2015) and since then presumably adopted in the community for comparability

Proceedings of the Second Workshop on Advances in Language and Vision Research, pages 22–28
©2021 Association for Computational Linguistics

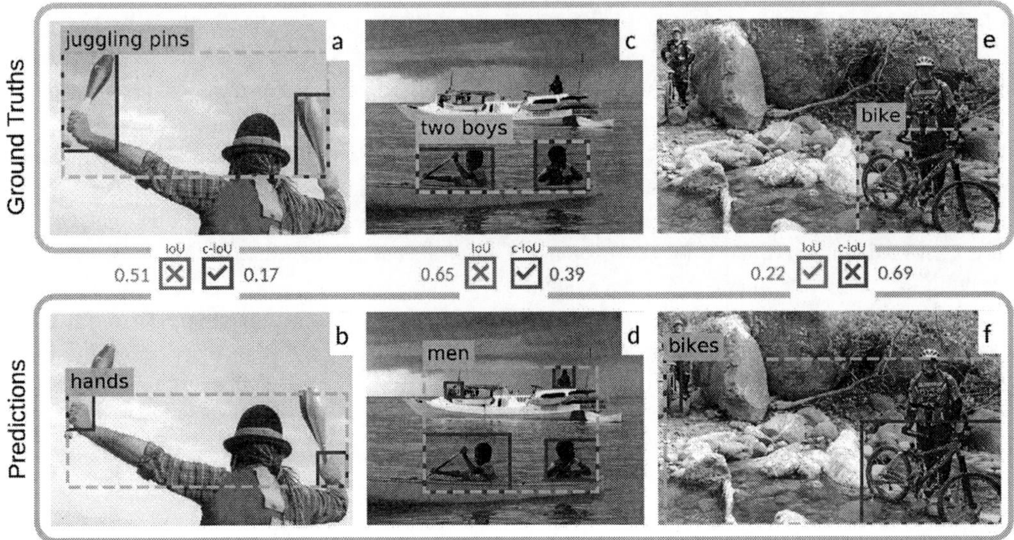

Figure 2: Ground truth (green/top) and prediction (orange/bottom) cases with components (blue) and union boxes (dashed). The Ground Truth box label in green represents the phrase being grounded; the orange phrase marked in the prediction represents the concept fitting the detected plural object. The scores represent the IoU score (red, left) and the c-IoU score (blue, right), respectively. Predictions with scores ≥ 0.5 are considered correct. The check boxes show whether the metrics correctly evaluate the prediction. For example, for sub-figures (a+b) the c-IoU score is 0.17 and so the prediction is considered incorrect (≤ 0.5), thus the c-IoU metric correctly evaluates that the detected *hands* constitute an incorrect prediction for *juggling pins* (blue tick).

quality mappings for all phrase types. However, the annotation of plural phrases is challenging, as shown in Testoni et al. (2020); Marín et al. (2020) who investigate how phrases can refer to groups of objects or several entities within a group.

(Semi-)supervised PG systems generally do not differentiate singular and plural phrases and always predict a single box (Li et al., 2019; Lu et al., 2020; Plummer et al., 2015). For multiple boxes with the same predicted label, either the largest box or the union box is returned. Thus, components are not individually evaluated, and the same metric, *Intersection over Union (IoU)*, can be uniformly applied to a prediction box for any phrase type. IoU computes the ratio of the *area of overlap* over the *area of union* between a predicted and a gold box and is usually thresholded at IoU ≥ 0.5.

While IoU is a simple and effective metric for evaluating 1:1 mappings, we claim that it is unsuitable for evaluating plural phrases. We show that the union box is in fact not an ideal gold representation for plural phrases: it can make the gold box overly large, especially when including areas that do not represent any components, and thus introduces an evaluation bias favoring large prediction boxes. Our contributions are as follows:

i) We detect, describe and *quantify an evaluation bias* in the grounding of plural phrases when applying standard practice of measuring *IoU* over *union boxes*, using an unsupervised PG system on the PG dataset Flickr30k.

ii) We propose a *novel evaluation metric* based on component boxes rather than union boxes.

iii) We show that the *new metric alleviates this bias* and reduces the evaluation failures.

2   Evaluation Bias

IoU is the standard evaluation metric used in PG and rewards predictions that highly overlap with their gold boxes. For a *plural phrase* that links to multiple ground truth boxes, a *union box* enclosing all components is generated, so the same evaluation metric can be used for singular and plural phrase types. However, we argue that this method introduces a considerable bias, which may result in unfair evaluations. When evaluating on union boxes, we ignore all information about the components' sizes and positions, and only consider the union box outline. If components are spread across the image, a union box can become much larger than the combined size of its component boxes, which makes them imprecise and ambiguous.

Figures (2.a) vs. (2.b) show an example of two-component union boxes that are highly overlapping – one for *pins*, the other for *hands*. Hence, a system that returns the prediction (2.b) for *juggling pins* will be unduly considered as correct. Similarly, for a prediction with too few or too many components, IoU often fails to detect such mistakes, as in (2.c) vs. (2.d). The ground truth (2.c) for *two boys* includes only two components, yet a system predicting four components (including the men on the boat) will still be correct according to IoU.

This type of 'false positive' arises from the generation of *union boxes*, in conjunction with the relatively forgiving nature of the IoU metric for large predicted boxes. Given such undesirable failure cases, we conjecture that IoU can lead to unwanted evaluation biases and we investigate whether it is a sound metric for evaluating plural phrases.

2.1 Quantifying the Bias

We verify and quantify the potential evaluation bias on GT annotations of Flickr30k and empirical system predictions. Depending on the distribution of component boxes across the image, the union box can be large, even if the components themselves are small. In Fig. (2.a) 75.47% of the union box area does not represent any component, so we term this area *filler space*. On the complete Flickr30k data, we compute an average of 3.6 components per plural phrase, which on average cover only 68% of the union box area, leaving one third (32%) of the space unfilled. For 24% of all union boxes, the filler space covers more than 50%, the gold box being twice as large as its components.

Hence, there is considerable potential for an evaluation bias to arise, as the IoU metric may unfairly favor large prediction boxes in two ways: i) overly large union boxes allow the prediction of wrong object types that happen to fall into the gold union box area; and ii) even if objects of the correct type are predicted, a large union box may be filled with too many or too few objects compared to the GT, and may still satisfy IoU ≥ 0.5. To verify this hypothesis, we perform experiments using an unsupervised PG system, capable of processing plural phrases.

2.2 Bias in Context of System Performance

Most existing PG systems are (semi-)supervised learners and need to be adapted to the special case of plural phrases: their object detectors need to deliver union boxes, instead of single-object boxes. Since plural phrases are much less frequent than singular phrases, this distributional bias may lead to poorer predictions for plural phrases. Recently, unsupervised PG systems have been proposed (Wang and Specia, 2019; Parcalabescu and Frank, 2020) that achieve competitive performance, but are not subject to such frequency biases. We thus perform our experiments with a system that replicates Wang and Specia (2019)'s approach.

The system[2] maps phrases to predicted bounding boxes using similarity rankings derived from word embeddings for the phrase and the candidate box labels. Since our object detector only detects single objects, we automatically generate plural objects that include several objects, by combining boxes with the same label.

We apply the system to a test set of 10k images with 5 captions each, containing 3.3 phrases on average. We ground ca. 141k phrases, including ca. 31k plural phrases (21.8%) and measure accuracy for the predicted bounding box(es) for a given phrase, using the IoU evaluation metric (with a threshold at 0.5) as success criterion.

Table (1.a) displays evaluation results for *all phrases* vs. *plural phrases* only, and in both cases we distinguish predicted boxes comprising *single* objects only vs. *all* objects (single and plural), for various settings: i) *upper bound* (row 1); ii) performance of our PG system in different settings (rows 2-4); and iii) manipulated predictions, i.e. *max box* and *random predictions* (rows 5-6).

i) Upper bound *Upper bound* represents the highest possible PG performance, computed as percentage of phrases with at least one detected object that matches the GT. Using only *single* objects, we find an upper bound of 72.34 for all phrases and 46.67 for plural phrases. The fact that single objects – which cannot constitute correct groundings for plural phrases – provide 'successful candidates' for nearly half the plural phrases, emphasizes that IoU is not a suitable metric for plural phrase grounding. When considering boxes with multiple objects as candidates, the upper bound increases by 2.82 percentage points (pp.) to 75.16 on all phrases and by 20.98 pp. to 67.65 on plural phrases, demonstrating that *plural objects* are an essential addition.

ii) PG system evaluation This setting also shows an increase when considering *plural objects*, with an increase for *all phrases* by 1.69 pp., and for *plural phrases* by 5.45 pp. Candidate pruning fur-

---

[2]Details of the system are given in the Appendix.

a) IoU metric	All Phrases		Plural Phrases		b) c-IoU metric	All Phrases		Plural Phrases	
	single	*all*	*single*	*all*		*single*	*all*	*single*	*all*
Upper bound [+prun.]	72.34	75.16	46.67	67.65	Upper bound [+prun.]	72.34	73.69	46.69	60.94
Unsupervised PG	47.94	49.63	31.15	36.60	Unsupervised PG	48.05	49.94	31.00	37.37
– [+pruning]	-	53.36	-	56.46	– [+pruning]	-	52.38	-	50.09
– [+pruning, +enlarged]	47.99	52.03	33.84	52.45	– [+pruning, +enlarged]	47.26	51.02	29.84	46.95
Max box predictions	23.63	23.63	32.19	32.19	Max box predictions	21.45	20.98	22.88	22.19
Random predictions	17.97	20.75	24.09	29.17	Random predictions	9.17	13.86	7.62	14.08

Table 1: PG performance in accuracy computed with **IoU** vs. **c-IoU** on *all* vs. *plural phrases*, considering *single* object boxes vs. *all* (single & multiple) object boxes. +*pruning* filters candidates: for plural phrases we consider plural objects only; for singular phrases only single objects. +*enlarged*: size of detected objs. increased by 50%.

ther increases accuracy by 3.73 pp. on *all phrases* and 19.86 pp. on *plural phrases*, while limiting the potential exploitation of large candidate boxes.

iii) Manipulated predictions We hypothesized that using IoU with union boxes is too forgiving and favors large predictions, so we conduct experiments where we generate overly large object predictions: in one, predictions cover the entire image (*max box predictions*); in the other, original predictions are enlarged by 50%. For the *max box predictions*, we obtain overall 23% correct predictions, and 32% for *plural phrases*. Thus, every third plural phrase benefits from very large prediction boxes. Ideally, IoU is designed to punish predictions that are overly large or not well placed over the gold box, due to division by union area. However, the image frame limits the maximum box size to the size of the image, which reduces the normalization effect for large objects.

Measuring PG performance with enlarged prediction boxes [+enlarged], increases accuracy by 2.69 pp. for *plural phrases* when considering singular objects only – despite singular objects being unsuitable predictions by definition. This further supports our hypothesis that large predictions are generally favored. However, larger predictions do not increase performance on mixed phrase types, so singular phrases must be less affected by this bias. For plural objects, PG performance even decreases with enlarged predictions, which suggests that plural objects cannot benefit from expansion.

In sum, the high upper bound with singular objects for plural phrases, the strong performance when predicting the entire image, and the effect on PG performance when enlarging prediction boxes all support our hypothesis that *the evaluation of plural phrases by IoU is biased*. Hence, a new metric is needed to counter this bias.

3 Our new Evaluation Metric c-IoU

We aim at a metric that is not based on the union box, but its components. However – any metric is only as good as the quality of its underlying ground truth. When studying the annotation of plural phrases in Flickr30k, we found that many of them are imprecise or incomplete. Nearly one third of plural phrases are annotated with a single bounding box without components and for 9% the number of components does not match the cardinality of the referring phrase (e.g. two component boxes for *three women*), leaving 37% of the plural phrases without proper representation of their components. This high level of noise precludes any metric that relies on matching the number of component boxes of ground truth and predictions.

In §2.1 we identified the filler space of union boxes – jointly with IoU evaluation – as the source of the detected evaluation bias. To combat this, we define an *adapted IoU* that is not computed over the union box, but its *aggregated components*, by taking the intersection of all gold and predicted component boxes and dividing by the area of the union of all (gold and predicted) component boxes. We call this metric *component IoU (c-IoU)*. c-IoU is analogous to standard IoU for single-object boxes, and only affects the evaluation of plural phrases, as seen in Fig. (1). By considering the area covered by *all* component boxes, it gains robustness against annotation noise.

Fig. (2.a-d) show two examples where IoU fails to correctly evaluate predictions, while c-IoU succeeds. The prediction *hands* for the phrase *juggling pins* yields an IoU score of 0.51, which accepts the prediction. The c-IoU score of 0.17, by contrast, rejects this prediction. Similarly, the prediction *men* is considered correct for *two boys* by IoU (0.65), but correctly rejected by c-IoU (0.39).

4 Evaluation of Component IoU (c-IoU)

We evaluate **c-IoU** in the same way as we did in §2.2 to quantify biases under IoU, and give results in Table (1.b). We expect c-IoU to avoid biases for plurals and ensuing false predictions.

The experiments confirm our expectation: large prediction boxes yield lower scores with c-IoU. *Max box predictions*, computed on all objects found in the image, yields 9.31 pp. lower accuracy on plural phrases. PG system performance with enlarged predictions measured on singular objects for plural phrases increases by 2.69 pp. to 33.84 for IoU, yet decreases by 1.16 pp. to 29.84 for c-IoU. Therefore, c-IoU better detects wrong predictions.

But c-IoU does not catch all incorrect predictions: with pruning, accuracy measured with c-IoU increases less (+12.72 pp. to 50.09) compared to IoU (+19.86 pp. to 56.46). Data inspection shows that without pruning, c-IoU allows plural objects for singular phrases (and vice versa) – typically the plural object includes the targeted object plus another small object in the background (see Fig. (2.e+f)). Since the background object drastically expands the union box but not the component union area, IoU may correctly evaluate such cases, while c-IoU could fail. Hence, a combination of both metrics could be beneficial, where c-IoU ensures that the right components are selected, while IoU may detect out-of-focus objects.

As a final test, we evaluate both metrics on artificially generated false plural box predictions. For each phrase, we assemble a *random prediction* consisting of 2-5 components with different labels. Ideally, most predictions should be labeled as incorrect, thus a lower accuracy indicates a more sensitive metric. c-IoU indeed returns much lower scores than IoU: 9.17 and 7.62 (c-IoU) vs. 19.97 and 24.09 (IoU) on *all phrases* and *plural phrases*, showing that c-IoU effectively counters the bias.

5 Conclusion

We have detected, described and quantified an evaluation bias for plural phrases in the PG literature. Our alternative c-IoU metric, acting on components rather than union boxes, alleviates this bias, as we show in experiments with an unsupervised PG system. Future work could test more systems to assess by how much state-of-the-art performance is lower than currently estimated. Evaluation of plural phrases is further impeded by the low quality of the gold boxes. Therefore, future benchmarks need to annotate plural phrases with all their components if we wish to enable PG systems to better learn the intricacies of language (including plural expressions) in relation to the visual modality.

References

Mark Everingham, Luc Van Gool, Christopher KI Williams, John Winn, and Andrew Zisserman. 2010. The pascal visual object classes (voc) challenge. *International journal of computer vision*, 88(2):303–338.

Nikolai Ilinykh, Sina Zarrieß, and David Schlangen. 2019. Tell me more: A dataset of visual scene description sequences. In *Proceedings of the 12th International Conference on Natural Language Generation*, pages 152–157.

Sahar Kazemzadeh, Vicente Ordonez, Mark Matten, and Tamara Berg. 2014. ReferItGame: Referring to Objects in Photographs of Natural Scenes. In *Proceedings of the 2014 conference on empirical methods in natural language processing (EMNLP)*, pages 787–798.

Ranjay Krishna, Yuke Zhu, Oliver Groth, Justin Johnson, Kenji Hata, Joshua Kravitz, Stephanie Chen, Yannis Kalantidis, Li-Jia Li, David A Shamma, et al. 2017. Visual Genome: Connecting Language and Vision using Crowdsourced Dense Image Annotations. *International journal of computer vision*, 123(1):32–73.

Liunian Harold Li, Mark Yatskar, Da Yin, Cho-Jui Hsieh, and Kai-Wei Chang. 2019. VisualBERT: A Simple and Performant Baseline for Vision and Language. *arXiv preprint arXiv:1908.03557*.

Tsung-Yi Lin, Michael Maire, Serge Belongie, James Hays, Pietro Perona, Deva Ramanan, Piotr Dollár, and C Lawrence Zitnick. 2014. Microsoft COCO: Common objects in context. In *European conference on computer vision*, pages 740–755. Springer.

Jiasen Lu, Vedanuj Goswami, Marcus Rohrbach, Devi Parikh, and Stefan Lee. 2020. 12-in-1: Multi-task vision and language representation learning. In *Proceedings of the IEEE/CVF Conference on Computer Vision and Pattern Recognition*, pages 10437–10446.

Nicolás Marín, Gustavo Rivas-Gervilla, and Daniel Sánchez. 2020. A preliminary approach to referring to groups of objects in images. In *2020 IEEE International Conference on Fuzzy Systems (FUZZ-IEEE)*, pages 1–7. IEEE.

Tomas Mikolov, Ilya Sutskever, Kai Chen, Greg S Corrado, and Jeff Dean. 2013. Distributed representations of words and phrases and their compositionality. In *Advances in neural information processing systems*, pages 3111–3119.

Letitia Parcalabescu and Anette Frank. 2020. Exploring Phrase Grounding Without Training: Contextualisation and Extension to Text-Based Image Retrieval. In *Proceedings of the IEEE/CVF Conference on Computer Vision and Pattern Recognition Workshops*, pages 962–963.

Bryan A Plummer, Liwei Wang, Chris M Cervantes, Juan C Caicedo, Julia Hockenmaier, and Svetlana Lazebnik. 2015. Flickr30k Entities: Collecting region-to-phrase correspondences for richer image-to-sentence models. In *Proceedings of the IEEE international conference on computer vision*, pages 2641–2649.

Alberto Testoni, Claudio Greco, Tobias Bianchi, Mauricio Mazuecos, Agata Marcante, Luciana Benotti, and Raffaella Bernardi. 2020. They are not all alike: Answering different spatial questions requires different grounding strategies. In *Proceedings of the Third International Workshop on Spatial Language Understanding*, pages 29–38.

Josiah Wang and Lucia Specia. 2019. Phrase Localization Without Paired Training Examples. In *Proceedings of the IEEE International Conference on Computer Vision*, pages 4663–4672.

A Appendix

System details Our approach replicates the unsupervised *bag-of-objects approach* by Wang and Specia (2019). The phrase and the labels for candidate objects are embedded using 300-dimensional word2vec embeddings (Mikolov et al., 2013). The object candidates are ranked by their *cosine similarity* to the phrase, and the object with the most similar label is returned. If there are several objects for the highest ranking label, we return the largest one in case of singular phrases and the union box (plural object) in case of plural phrases. In contrast to prior systems that used (multiple) object detectors with large label sets (545 or 1600 labels), our object detector, trained on Visual Genome (Krishna et al., 2017), uses only 150 coarse-grained labels.

We test performance on the Flickr30k Entities (Plummer et al., 2015) dataset for phrase grounding. The test set consists of 10k images with 5 captions each, containing 3.3 phrases on average. We ground 140 972 phrases, including 30 762 plural phrases (21.8%). The vocabulary of the phrases is relatively diverse with 8301 different words on the test split.

Evaluation examples Fig. (3) shows a few more examples of ground truths and our system's predictions, as well as the correctness of the evaluation using IoU and c-IoU. Fig. (3.a-d) show examples where IoU accepts predictions with incorrect object labels, while c-IoU rejects them. In (3.e+f), c-IoU finds that two hats are missing while IoU accepts the incomplete prediction. For example (3.g+h), c-IoU fails to identify that the prediction has a missing component. IoU correctly evaluates the prediction as incorrect because of the obvious union box difference, which makes the IoU drop below 0.5. Example (3.i+j) is a challenging case, as the phrase [*two young men clutch rags in*] ***their hands*** requires context for correct grounding, which is not provided by a PG system that looks at phrases individually. As expected, our system additionally predicts the old man's hand, which is incorrect but since the superfluous hand has a small area and is located closely to the others, both evaluation metrics fail to detect this mistake. Finally, in (3.k+l) the ground truth is missing the annotation of the components, so that c-IoU cannot correctly evaluate this correct prediction.

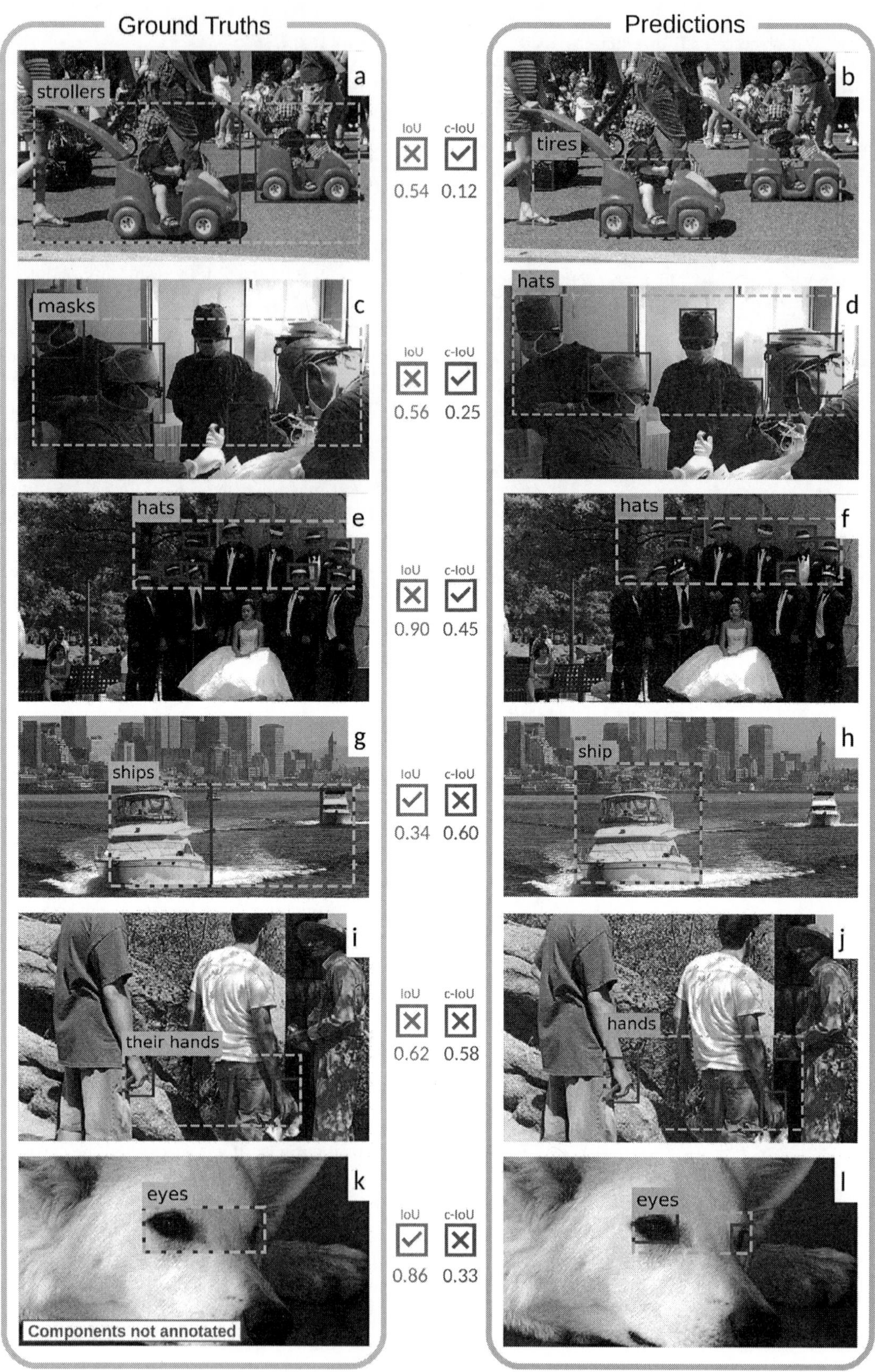

Figure 3: GT and prediction cases with union boxes (dashed) and components (blue); the check marks show whether IoU (red) and c-IoU (blue) correctly evaluate the prediction (for further explanation see Figure 2).

PanGEA: The Panoramic Graph Environment Annotation Toolkit

Alexander Ku[*] **Peter Anderson**[*] **Jordi Pont-Tuset** **Jason Baldridge**
Google Research
{alexku, pjand, jponttuset, jridge}@google.com

Abstract

PanGEA, the Panoramic Graph Environment Annotation toolkit, is a lightweight toolkit for collecting speech and text annotations in photo-realistic 3D environments. PanGEA immerses annotators in a web-based simulation and allows them to move around easily as they speak and/or listen. It includes database and cloud storage integration, plus utilities for automatically aligning recorded speech with manual transcriptions and the virtual pose of the annotators. Out of the box, PanGEA supports two tasks – collecting navigation instructions and navigation instruction following – and it could be easily adapted for annotating walking tours, finding and labeling landmarks or objects, and similar tasks. We share best practices learned from using PanGEA in a 20,000 hour annotation effort to collect the Room-Across-Room dataset. We hope that our open-source annotation toolkit and insights will both expedite future data collection efforts and spur innovation on the kinds of grounded language tasks such environments can support.

1 Introduction

The release of high-quality 3D building and street captures (Chang et al., 2017; Mirowski et al., 2019; Mehta et al., 2020; Xia et al., 2018; Straub et al., 2019) has galvanized interest in developing embodied navigation agents that can operate in complex human environments. Based on these environments, annotations have been collected for a variety of tasks including navigating to a particular class of object (ObjectNav) (Batra et al., 2020), navigating from language instructions aka vision-and-language navigation (VLN) (Anderson et al., 2018b; Chen et al., 2019; Qi et al., 2020; Ku et al., 2020), and vision-and-dialog navigation (Thomason et al., 2020; Hahn et al., 2020). To date, most of these data collection efforts have required the development of custom annotation tools.

To expedite future data collection efforts, in this paper we introduce PanGEA, an open-sourced annotation toolkit designed for these settings.[1] Specifically, PanGEA assumes an environment represented by discrete navigation graphs connecting high-resolution 360° panoramas, where each node represents a unique viewpoint in the environment and actions involve moving between these viewpoints. Examples of suitable environments include the indoor buildings from Matterport3D (Chang et al., 2017) (using the navigation graphs from Anderson et al. (2018b)) and the street-level environments from StreetLearn (Mirowski et al., 2019).

Out of the box, PanGEA supports two annotation modes: the *Guide* task and the *Follower* task. In the Guide task, Guides look around and move through an environment to follow a pre-defined path and attempt to create a navigation instruction for others to follow. In the Follower task, annotators listen to a Guide's instructions and attempt to follow the path. These annotation modes are based on the Vision-and-Language Navigation (VLN) setting proposed by Anderson et al. (2018b). However, compared to similar annotation tools, PanGEA includes substantial additional capabilities, notably:

- annotation via voice recording (in addition to text entry)
- virtual pose tracking to record what annotators look at
- utilities for aligning a transcript of the words heard or uttered by each annotator with their visual perceptions and actions
- integration with cloud database and storage platforms
- a modular API facilitating easy extension to new tasks and new environments

PanGEA has already been used in two papers. It was used to collect Room-Across-Room (RxR) (Ku et al., 2020), a dataset of human-annotated navigation instructions in English, Hindi and Telugu

---

[*]First two authors contributed equally.

[1]github.com/google-research/pangea

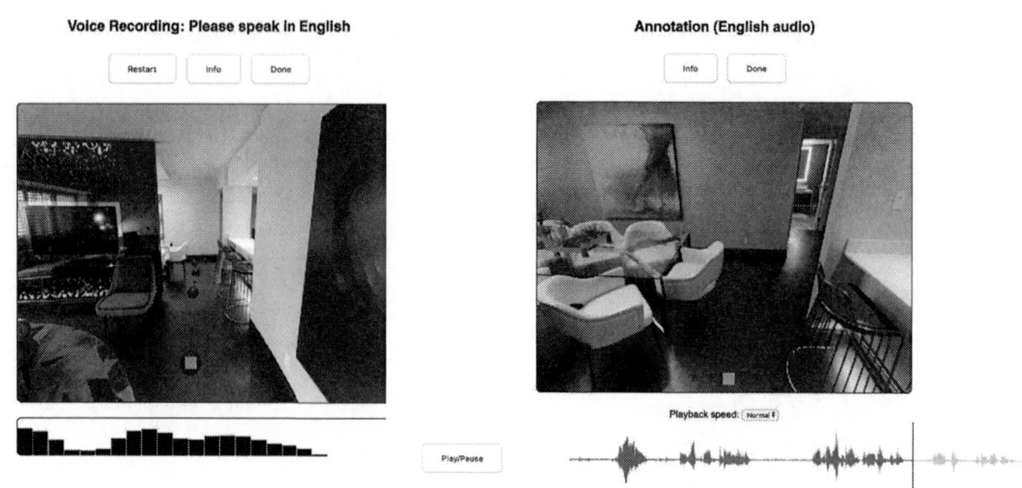

Figure 1: Screenshots of the PanGEA Guide and Follower interfaces. In the Guide task (left), Guides explore a given path while attempting to create a navigation instruction for others to follow. Guides can pause and restart the audio recording at any time. After recording is completed, Guides transcribe their own audio. In the Follower task (right), annotators listen to a Guide's instructions and attempt to follow the intended path. Followers can skip around the Guide's audio using the audio waveform at bottom right. In both tasks, PanGEA tracks the annotators virtual camera pose and automatically aligns it with the Guide's audio transcript.

which is the largest VLN dataset by an order of magnitude. PanGEA was also used to perform human evaluations of model-generated navigation instructions in Zhao et al. (2021). It could be trivially adapted to other tasks that combine annotation with movement, such as annotating walking tours, or finding and labeling particular landmarks or objects.

We next describe PanGEA's capabitilies in more detail. In the final section we share some best practices learned from using PanGEA to collect RxR, which required more than 20,000 annotation hours.

2   PanGEA Toolkit

Guide Task   In the Guide task (Figure 1, left), Guides look around and move to explore an environment while recording an audio narration. For the RxR data collection, the Guide's movement was restricted to a particular path through the environment, and annotators were instructed to record navigation instructions that would be sufficiently descriptive for others to follow the same path. However, this restriction can be relaxed to allow free movement and narration for other purposes. Once the Guide is satisfied with their recording, they are asked to manually transcribe their own voice recording into text. This ensures high quality tran-

scription results.

During the Guide task, in parallel to the annotator's voice recording, PanGEA captures a timestamped record of the annotator's virtual camera movements, which we call a *pose trace*. By default, PanGEA is configured to use Firebase[2], saving the Guide's audio recording to a cloud storage bucket, and the transcript, pose trace and other metadata to a cloud database for post processing. Inspired by Localized Narratives (Pont-Tuset et al., 2020), PanGEA includes a utility to automatically align each Guide's pose trace with the manual transcript of their audio recording. This is achieved by using a Speech to Text service[3] to first generate a noisy-but-timestamped automatic transcription. PanGEA then using dynamic time warping to align tokens in the automatic transcript to the manual transcript before propagating timestamps from the automatic to the manual transcription (Figure 2). The result is fine-grained synchronization between the transcribed text, the pixels seen, and the actions taken by the Guide.

Follower Task   In the Follower task (Figure 1, right), Followers begin at a specified starting point in an environment and are asked to follow a Guide's

---

[2] `https://firebase.google.com`
[3] `https://cloud.google.com/`
`speech-to-text`

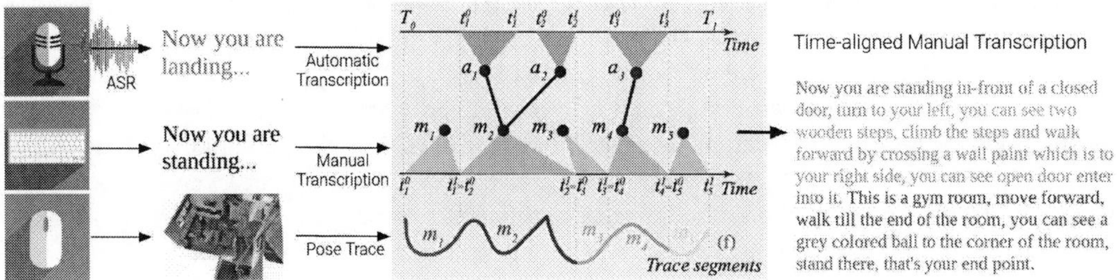

Figure 2: PanGEA time-aligns each annotators manual audio transcription (middle) to a *pose trace* recording their virtual camera movements (bottom). This is achieved by first generating a noisy-but-timestamped automatic transcription (top), which is aligned with the manual transcription using dynamic time warping in order to propagate timestamps to the manual transcription. Figure adapted from Pont-Tuset et al. (2020)

instructions. They observe the environment and navigate as the Guide's audio plays. Followers can skip forward or backward in the audio recording by clicking on an audio waveform representation of the Guide's recording. This allows them to skip over periods of silence or to listen to part of the audio again. Once the Follower believes they have reached the the end of the path, or they give up, they indicate they are done and the task ends. Note that although the Follower task supports audio instructions, it can be easily adapted to replace the audio instruction with a textual instruction. This was the approach taken by Zhao et al. (2021).

As with the Guide task, the Follower's pose trace is recorded and saved to a cloud database, along with the timestamp of the Guide's audio that the Follower listened to at each moment. This allows the Follower's visual percepts and actions to be accurately aligned with text tokens in the Guide's instructions. Similarity between the annotated (Guide) path and the Follower path is also a natural measure of the joint quality of both the Guide and the Follower annotations. In the experiments for RxR, the path extracted from the Follower's pose trace was also used as additional supervision when training Follower agents, since it represents a step-by-step account of how a human solved the task and the visual inputs they focused on in order to do so (Ku et al., 2020).

Deployment PanGEA comes with several demos using a very simplistic environment. To deploy PanGEA for a new large-scale collection effort requires completing 3 main steps:

- Creating a new app in Firebase to initialize the cloud storage and cloud database,
- Setting up an appropriate crowdsourcing plat-

form to serve the PanGEA front-end to a pool of annotators, and
- Setting up the environment to be used, e.g., hosting the images and navigation graphs in a storage bucket in an appropriate format.

Further details are provided in the PanGEA readme.

3   Observations and Best Practices

PanGEA was developed for the collection of the RxR dataset, a 20,000+ hour annotation effort based on Matterport3D indoor scenes. Many of the lessons learned during this collection effort are codified in the PanGEA toolkit. For example, we found that uploading recorded audio at the end of the Guide task was time consuming, and so in the final version of PanGEA the wav file is uploaded in the background while the annotator is busy transcribing their audio. We also found that audio annotations could include long periods of silence, so we provided Follower annotators with an audio waveform visualization and an interface to skip over silence. Some other observations and best practices for reducing annotation times and improving annotation quality are shared in this section.

Annotators Complete Tasks in Creative Ways PanGEA is designed to capture the alignment between annotators' visual percepts, actions and utterances to provide fine-grained spatio-temporal grounding. In initial trials with PanGEA, we found that some annotators – with the best of intentions – completely undermined this paradigm. We had envisioned them speaking while moving and looking at the environment; however, in an effort to generate more fluent instructions, some annotators first explored the environment while drafting a navigation instruction separately in a text editor. Then, having finalized the textual instruction, the annotator read it all at the end of the audio recording. While this strategy indeed produced high-quality navigation instructions, the instructions were no longer time-aligned to the pose trace. Interestingly, the language used in the instructions also differed. Instructions drafted as text tended to use more connective phrases — for example, "turn right *and then* you will see a dining table" instead of "turn right... *now* you see a dining table". We found it challenging to add guardrails in PanGEA that could prevent this behaviour without unduly restricting the freedom of the annotators and the flexibility of the toolkit. Instead, we addressed this issue–successfully–via explicit training.

Annotator Training   To overcome the aforementioned issue and to improve annotation quality in general, for RxR, we conducted an interactive virtual training session with annotators, providing examples of ideal annotations and various failure modes. Annotators were also able to ask questions regarding how to best complete the tasks assigned to them. Although interactive training sessions are not always possible, at minimum we recommend providing annotators with a training video that shows a walk-through of the task and notes common pitfalls to avoid. We provide links to the demo videos for the RxR Guide task[4] and Follower task[5] (initially called the Tourist task).

Pilot Collections and Learning Periods   Annotating and following navigation instructions in a virtual world is a complex task. We recommend allowing for several small-scale pilot data collections to identify issues with the collection process. This includes having the team creating the dataset perform the tasks using the tool. Secondly, we recommend allowing for a learning period whenever a new annotator is introduced to the task, i.e., planning to discard the first 5–10 annotations produced by a new annotator. We found that rotating annotators between both Guide and Follower tasks early in their experience improved annotation quality because doing so provides much greater awareness of the needs of Followers when completing the Guide tasks.

Data Monitoring Dashboard   We recommend using VLN evaluation metrics such as success rate, navigation error and SPL (Anderson et al., 2018a) (or similar metrics for alternative tasks) to continually monitor the quality of the collected Guide navigation instructions and Follower paths. By storing the collected annotations in Firebase, it is relatively easy to construct web-based interfaces to monitor these metrics. In the case of RxR, we created a monitoring dashboard that displayed success rates for each annotator pool and also each annotator, with the capability to replay the pose traces from individual Guide and Follower annotations. Annotators were able to see an anonymized view on their progress as it related to others, which helped them assess whether they were performing the task correctly or needed additional changes and perhaps explicit guidance.

Speech versus Writing   In tasks that require a person to perform actions while producing or comprehending language, it is much easier if people are allowed to use speech rather than writing because it allows them to use their hands and eyes fully for performing actions. This has very real consequences for thinking about future data collection efforts. Speech interactions will be essential for any tasks that include time pressure, such as collaborative games where players use language to coordinate. There is also a simple but significant cost advantage: on average, the transcription portion for an RxR Guide annotation took three to four times longer than collecting the speech instruction itself, so either a great deal more instructions could have been collected, or the cost could have been significantly reduced. Speech also encodes intonation and is more likely to elicit interesting dialectal differences. For these and other reasons, we may thus want to encourage more research that works on language grounding tasks that work with speech directly, and provide current best automatic speech recognition output for those who insist on working with text only.

4   Future Applications

There are many potential future applications of PanGEA and tools that could be built based on the design decisions discussed above. We are particularly excited about multi-agent problems that collect pose traces from multiple participants as they coordinate via language, such as hide and seek games or tasks where items must be moved from one location to another to satisfy goals or solve puzzles, similar to CerealBar (Suhr et al., 2019).

---

[4]https://youtu.be/aJkJfB8oI2M
[5]https://youtu.be/vcP-oX1t0CU

References

Peter Anderson, Angel Chang, Devendra Singh Chaplot, Alexey Dosovitskiy, Saurabh Gupta, Vladlen Koltun, Jana Kosecka, Jitendra Malik, Roozbeh Mottaghi, Manolis Savva, and Amir R. Zamir. 2018a. On evaluation of embodied navigation agents. *arXiv preprint arXiv:1807.06757*.

Peter Anderson, Qi Wu, Damien Teney, Jake Bruce, Mark Johnson, Niko Sünderhauf, Ian Reid, Stephen Gould, and Anton van den Hengel. 2018b. Vision-and-language navigation: Interpreting visually-grounded navigation instructions in real environments. In *CVPR*, pages 3674–3683.

Dhruv Batra, Aaron Gokaslan, Aniruddha Kembhavi, Oleksandr Maksymets, Roozbeh Mottaghi, Manolis Savva, Alexander Toshev, and Erik Wijmans. 2020. Objectnav revisited: On evaluation of embodied agents navigating to objects. *arXiv preprint arXiv:2006.13171*.

Angel Chang, Angela Dai, Thomas Funkhouser, Maciej Halber, Matthias Niessner, Manolis Savva, Shuran Song, Andy Zeng, and Yinda Zhang. 2017. Matterport3d: Learning from RGB-D data in indoor environments. *International Conference on 3D Vision (3DV)*.

Howard Chen, Alane Suhr, Dipendra Misra, Noah Snavely, and Yoav Artzi. 2019. Touchdown: Natural language navigation and spatial reasoning in visual street environments. In *CVPR*.

Meera Hahn, Jacob Krantz, Dhruv Batra, Devi Parikh, James M. Rehg, Stefan Lee, and Peter Anderson. 2020. Where are you? localization from embodied dialog.

Alexander Ku, Peter Anderson, Roma Patel, Eugene Ie, and Jason Baldridge. 2020. Room-across-room: Multilingual vision-and-language navigation with dense spatiotemporal grounding. *EMNLP*.

Harsh Mehta, Yoav Artzi, Jason Baldridge, Eugene Ie, and Piotr Mirowski. 2020. Retouchdown: Adding touchdown to streetlearn as a shareable resource for language grounding tasks in street view. *EMNLP Workshop on Spatial Language Understanding (SpLU)*.

Piotr Mirowski, Andras Banki-Horvath, Keith Anderson, Denis Teplyashin, Karl Moritz Hermann, Mateusz Malinowski, Matthew Koichi Grimes, Karen Simonyan, Koray Kavukcuoglu, Andrew Zisserman, et al. 2019. The streetlearn environment and dataset. *arXiv preprint arXiv:1903.01292*.

Jordi Pont-Tuset, Jasper Uijlings, Soravit Changpinyo, Radu Soricut, and Vittorio Ferrari. 2020. Connecting vision and language with localized narratives. In *ECCV*.

Yuankai Qi, Qi Wu, Peter Anderson, Xin Wang, William Yang Wang, Chunhua Shen, and Anton van den Hengel. 2020. Reverie: Remote embodied visual referring expression in real indoor environments. In *CVPR*.

Julian Straub, Thomas Whelan, Lingni Ma, Yufan Chen, Erik Wijmans, Simon Green, Jakob J. Engel, Raul Mur-Artal, Carl Ren, Shobhit Verma, Anton Clarkson, Mingfei Yan, Brian Budge, Yajie Yan, Xiaqing Pan, June Yon, Yuyang Zou, Kimberly Leon, Nigel Carter, Jesus Briales, Tyler Gillingham, Elias Mueggler, Luis Pesqueira, Manolis Savva, Dhruv Batra, Hauke M. Strasdat, Renzo De Nardi, Michael Goesele, Steven Lovegrove, and Richard Newcombe. 2019. The Replica dataset: A digital replica of indoor spaces. *arXiv preprint arXiv:1906.05797*.

Alane Suhr, Claudia Yan, Jack Schluger, Stanley Yu, Hadi Khader, Marwa Mouallem, Iris Zhang, and Yoav Artzi. 2019. Executing instructions in situated collaborative interactions. In *Proceedings of the 2019 Conference on Empirical Methods in Natural Language Processing and the 9th International Joint Conference on Natural Language Processing (EMNLP-IJCNLP)*, pages 2119–2130, Hong Kong, China. Association for Computational Linguistics.

Jesse Thomason, Michael Murray, Maya Cakmak, and Luke Zettlemoyer. 2020. Vision-and-dialog navigation. In *Conference on Robot Learning (CoRL)*, pages 394–406. PMLR.

Fei Xia, Amir R. Zamir, Zhi-Yang He, Alexander Sax, Jitendra Malik, and Silvio Savarese. 2018. Gibson env: real-world perception for embodied agents. In *CVPR*. IEEE.

Ming Zhao, Peter Anderson, Vihan Jain, Su Wang, Alex Ku, Jason Baldridge, and Eugene Ie. 2021. On the evaluation of vision-and-language navigation instructions. In *Conference of the European Chapter of the Association for Computational Linguistics (EACL)*.

Learning to Learn Semantic Factors in Heterogeneous Image Classification

Boyue Fan
University of Sheffield
United Kingdom

Zhenting Liu
Pasadena City college
United States

Abstract

Few-shot learning is to recognize novel classes with a few labeled samples per class. Although numerous meta-learning methods have made significant progress, they struggle to directly address the heterogeneity of training and evaluating task distributions, resulting in the domain shift problem when transitioning to new tasks with disjoint spaces. In this paper, we propose a novel method to deal with the heterogeneity. Specifically, by simulating class-difference domain shift during the meta-train phase, a bilevel optimization procedure is applied to learn a transferable representation space that can rapidly adapt to heterogeneous tasks. Experiments demonstrate the effectiveness of our proposed method.

1 Introduction

Deep learning methods are now widely used in diverse applications. However, their efficacy is largely contingent on a large amount of labelled data in the target task and domain of interest (Vaswani et al., 2017). Different from humans that can easily learn to accomplish new tasks with a few examples, it is difficult for machines to rapidly generalize to new concepts with very little supervision, which calls considerable attention to the challenging few-shot learning (FSL) setting. For example, few-shot classification problem requires models to classify unlabeled samples into novel classes with only a few labeled samples available for training (Finn et al., 2017). Commonly understood as learning to learn, meta-learning paradigm has made significant progress in FSL by transferring knowledge extracted from a collection of previous tasks (Vinyals et al., 2016; Snell et al., 2017). Such task-agnostic knowledge can contribute to the current testing task with optimizing learning algorithms. However, beyond its recent achievements, meta-learning still faces the problem of generalization.

In contrast to supervised machine learning methods which assume that training and testing data are sampled i.i.d. from the same distribution, FSL aims to learn to address tasks from different distributions with limited data. This refers to the realistic scenario that the label spaces of future testing tasks can not be obtained in advance and are often disjoint with the label spaces of training tasks. In experiments, this is actualized by splitting all categories in the dataset into non-overlapping base classes and novel classes, while training tasks are sampled from base classes and testing tasks are samples from novel classes. Therefore, due to the class label difference, meta-learning approaches suffer from natural heterogeneous distributions of tasks. As each task can be regarded as having a separate domain, it can be considered as a special case of domain shift that is extremely serious when a large gap of semantic relationship exists between base classes and novel classes.

As most of the current meta-learning approaches make a strong assumption that training tasks and testing tasks are drawn from the similar distributions and share the same characteristics, (Chen et al., 2019) has shown the limitations of existing approaches in cross-domain FSL scenarios where base classes and novel classes are from different datasets. However, few works have focused on this issue to improve existing approaches. For example, as a representative work of metric-based meta-learning, Prototypical Network (Snell et al., 2017) learns a metric space where embeddings of query samples in one class are close to the centroid of support samples in the same class, and far from centroids of other classes in the task. While Prototypical Network benefits from a simple but effective inductive bias, it lacks adaptation to new tasks or domains.

In this paper, we propose to improve such metric-based approaches with a bilevel optimization procedure. Specifically, we simulate class-difference-caused domain shift during meta-training by simultaneously sampling multiple tasks with non-

Proceedings of the Second Workshop on Advances in Language and Vision Research, pages 34–38
©2021 Association for Computational Linguistics

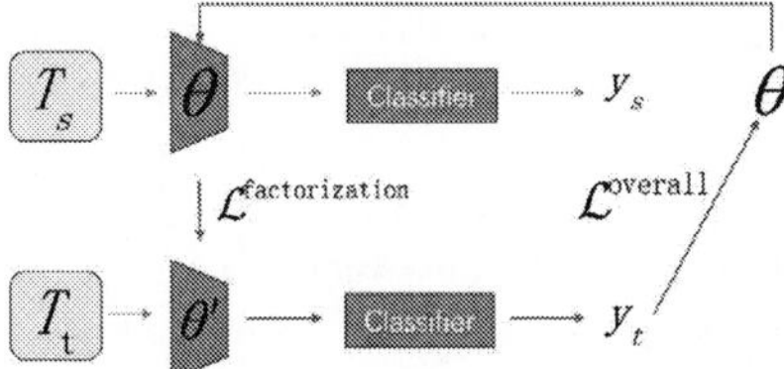

Figure 1: Overview of our proposed Meta-ProtoNet.

overlapping class sets. Each time one of the tasks is prepared as the target task for outer level optimization and the others are first used as the source tasks for inner level optimization of the network. Following this training strategy during the meta-train phase, the model can better adapt to the testing tasks from heterogeneous distributions with an adaptation step.

Moreover, different from some usual options of inner objective, we use Shannon entropy as an unsupervised factorization loss to constrain the learned representations as near-binary codes (Chang et al., 2019). This can be viewed as learning a discriminative latent factor space for each task where each factor can be interpreted as a latent attribute that is corresponding to abstract visual concepts.

To summarize, our main contributions are :1) considering the challenge of heterogeneous task distributions faced by few-shot learning, we simulate the class-difference-caused domain shift in the meta-train phase, and devise a metric-based meta-learning approach integrated with a bilevel optimization for better generalization; 2) we propose to utilize an unsupervised factorization loss as the inner objective, making representations to be near-binary codes that reduce the difficulty of classifier learning. Meanwhile, due to the bilevel optimization between heterogeneous few-shot tasks during meta-training, the model can rapidly learn the representation space for testing tasks; 3) We conduct extensive experiments and analysis to demonstrate that our approach effectively improves the performance and interpretability under both conventional and cross-domain few-shot settings without introducing additional architectures, and thus it can be regarded as a better baseline.

2 Methodology

2.1 Prototypical Network.

As a simple but effective model for FSL learning, Prototypical Network (ProtoNet) (Snell et al., 2017) use an embedding function f_θ with parameters θ to encode each sample into a representation vector. For each class c in the class set C of the task T , a prototype vector p_c is defined as the mean vector of the embedded support samples in the class, which can be expressed as $p_c = \frac{1}{|\mathcal{S}_c|} \sum_{(x_i,y_i)\in\mathcal{S}_c} f_\theta(x_i)$. When inferring, the probability over classes for a query sample x_i is a softmax over the inverse of squared Euclidean distances between the query representation and prototype vectors, expressed as $P_\theta(y_i = c \mid x_i) = \frac{\exp\left(-\|f_\theta(x_i)-p_c\|^2\right)}{\sum_{c'\in C}\exp\left(-\|f_\theta(x_i)-p_{c'}\|^2\right)}$. The classification loss is the sum of negative log-probability of each query sample in task T with its ground-truth class label: $\mathcal{L}^{\text{classification}}(\theta) = -\sum_{c\in C}\sum_{x_i\in\mathcal{Q}_c}\log P_\theta(y_i = c \mid x_i)$.

2.2 Learning Latent Factors

As the embedding function f_θ of Prototypical Network can be any deep neural network, it is often organized as a convolutional neural network (CNN) for image classification tasks. In our MetaProtoNet, we set the activation function of the last layer to Sigmoid function $\sigma(x) = \frac{1}{1+\exp(-x)}$ instead of the most commonly used ReLU function. This limits the scale of the learned representations $f_\theta(x_i) \in (0,1)^d$, where d denotes the dimension number of the representations. Deep architectures are capable of learning to extract useful information from the samples, and potentially construct representations as the composition of the local abstract concepts that are useful for downstream tasks. Therefore, Sigmoid activated outputs of f_θ can be viewed as multi-label predictions on latent factors, as the activation of each dimension closer to 0 or 1 can be interpreted as the corresponding visual attributes being present and absent. Moreover, Meta-ProtoNet constrains the learned representations to become near-binary codes by applying Shannon entropy as an unsupervised factorization loss, expressed as

$$\mathcal{L}^{\text{factorization}}(\theta) = -\sum_{x_i\in\{\mathcal{S},\mathcal{Q}\}} \langle f_\theta(x_i), \log(f_\theta(x_i))\rangle \tag{1}$$

where $\log(\cdot)$ is applied element-wise, and $\langle\cdot,\cdot\rangle$ denotes the vector inner product operation. This not only encourages the representations to become more interpretable but also decreases the uncertainty of latent factors discovery.

2.3 Training Meta-ProtoNet

According to (Snell et al., 2017), Prototypical Network can be re-interpreted as a linear classifier that is applied to the representations learned by the non-linear embedding function. With the improvement above, near-binary representations generated by the embedding function are expected to be preferable for the jointly learned linear classifier without sacrificing representation power and differentiable optimization for exactly binary codes (Li et al., 2017). However, it would result in a suboptimal representation space for heterogeneous testing tasks since the metric-based approach is no longer updated to adapt to new domains in the meta-test phase. To overcome the approaching domain shift problem, we devise a bilevel optimization procedure for a fast adaptation to the feature distribution in the new task.

Specifically, instead of randomly sampling a single task, we simultaneously sample m tasks $\mathcal{T}_{\text{set}} = \{\mathcal{T}_1, \cdots, \mathcal{T}_m\}$ without class overlap from the distribution over training tasks $p\left(\mathcal{T}^{tr}\right)$ in the metatrain stage. For each task in $\mathcal{T}_{\text{set}}$, we first denote it as the target task $\mathcal{T}_t$ and obtain a copy of the model parameters θ as θ', then θ' is updated by minimizing the factorization loss over each task $\mathcal{T}_s$ in the source tasks $\mathcal{T}_{\text{set}} - \mathcal{T}_t$. Each update of θ' can be expressed as

$$\theta' = \theta' - \alpha \nabla_{\theta'} \mathcal{L}^{factorization}\left(\theta'\right) \qquad (2)$$

where α is the inner learning rate. This is viewed as the inner level of the bilevel optimization procedure, and after all of $\mathcal{T}_s$ are used for the update of θ', we utilize $\mathcal{T}_t$ to optimize the model. Specifically, the model parameters θ are updated as follows:

$$\theta = \theta - \beta \nabla_{\theta} \mathcal{L}^{\text{overall}}\left(\theta'\right) \qquad (3)$$

where β is the outer learning rate. The meta-optimization is performed over the model parameters θ, whereas the objective $\mathcal{L}^{\text{overall}}\left(\theta'\right)$ is computed using the updated model parameters θ' and can be expressed as

$$\mathcal{L}^{\text{overall}}\left(\theta'\right) = \mathcal{L}^{\text{classification}}\left(\theta'\right) + \gamma \mathcal{L}^{\text{factorization}}\left(\theta'\right) \qquad (4)$$

where γ is the trade-off hyperparameter. The key idea underlying the algorithm is that to alleviate the class-difference-caused domain shift, the task-specific knowledge including semantic information of categories is decomposed into reusable low-level task-agnostic knowledge by transferring latent factors across heterogeneous tasks. Each round of bilevel optimization can be viewed as a simulation of the whole process including meta-train and meta-test: In the inner level (corresponding to the meta-train phase), we encourage the model to learn to generate latent factors for tasks drawn from the source distribution. As high performance of classification on these tasks is not necessary and may be detrimental to the classification of heterogeneous target tasks, the inner objective only aims to discover latent factors and does not include classification loss. Moreover, we expect the learned latent factor space to be transferable, and thus the learning process of the source tasks can promote the learning of heterogeneous tasks. Therefore, in the outer level (corresponding to the meta-test phase), the model is optimized with the overall loss including classification loss and factorization loss.

2.4 Testing Meta-ProtoNet

In the meta-test phase, when adapting to each new testing task $\mathcal{T}_j$, the trained parameters θ are updated to θ' using only one gradient descent step with the factorization loss over $\mathcal{T}_j$. Therefore, a task-specific latent factor space of $\mathcal{T}_j$ is learned. The evaluation metric (i.e., the classification accuracy) is calculated with the updated parameters θ'.

3 Experiments

Datasets. In this paper, we address the few-shot classification problem under both conventional and cross-domain FSL settings. These settings are conducted on three benchmark datasets: miniImageNet (Vinyals et al., 2016), Caltech-UCSD-Birds 200-2011 (CUB) (Wah et al., 2011), and SUN Attribute Database (SUN) (Patterson et al., 2014).

Experimental Settings. We conduct experiments on 5-way 1-shot and 5-way 5-shot settings, there are 15 query samples per class in each task. We report the average accuracy (%) and the corresponding 95% confidence interval over the 2000 tasks randomly sampled from novel classes. To fairly evaluate the original performance of each method, we use the same 4-layer ConvNet (Vinyals et al., 2016) as the backbone for all methods and do not adopt any data augmentation during training. All methods are trained via SGD with Adam (Kingma and Ba, 2014), and the initial learning rate is set to e^{-3}. For each method, models are trained for 40,000 tasks at most, and the best model on the vali-

Method	miniImageNet → CUB		miniImageNet → SUN		CUB → miniImageNet	
	5-way 1-shot	5-way 5-shot	5-way 1-shot	5-way 5-shot	5-way 1-shot	5-way 5-shot
Meta-Learner LSTM	23.77	30.58	25.52	32.14	22.58	28.18
MAML	40.29	53.01	46.07	59.08	33.36	41.58
Reptile	24.66	40.86	32.15	50.38	24.56	40.60
Matching Network	38.34	47.64	39.58	53.20	26.23	32.90
Prototypical Network	36.60	54.36	46.31	66.21	29.22	38.73
Relation Network	39.33	50.64	44.55	61.45	28.64	38.01
Baseline	24.16	32.73	25.49	37.15	22.98	28.41
Baseline++	29.40	40.48	30.44	41.71	23.41	25.82
Meta-ProtoNet	**40.61**	**56.12**	**49.38**	**68.80**	**33.58**	**43.83**

Table 1: Average accuracy (%) comparison to state-of-the-arts with 95% confidence intervals on 5-way classification tasks under the cross-domain FSL setting. Best results are displayed in boldface.

Method	miniImageNet		CUB		SUN	
	5-way 1-shot	5-way 5-shot	5-way 1-shot	5-way 5-shot	5-way 1-shot	5-way 5-shot
Meta-Learner LSTM	24.99	29.79	36.23	44.39	30.99	44.86
MAML	45.69	60.90	48.87	63.99	57.75	71.45
Reptile	26.59	39.87	27.21	42.35	28.30	51.62
Matching Network	47.63	56.28	53.06	62.19	55.02	62.57
Prototypical Network	46.15	65.56	48.21	57.80	55.70	67.32
Relation Network	47.64	63.65	52.76	64.71	58.29	72.15
Baseline	23.84	32.09	25.14	35.35	27.44	34.54
Baseline++	30.15	41.19	32.48	42.43	35.56	44.42
Meta-ProtoNet	**47.87**	**66.05**	**53.30**	**65.37**	**58.79**	**73.90**

Table 2: Average accuracy (%) comparison to state-of-the-arts with 95% confidence intervals on 5-way classification tasks under the conventional FSL setting. Best results are displayed in boldface.

dation classes is used to evaluate the final reporting performance in the meta-test phase.

Evaluation Using the Conventional Setting. Table 1 shows the comparative results under the conventional FSL setting on three benchmark datasets. It is observed that Meta-ProtoNet outperforms the original Prototypical Network in all conventional FSL scenarios. For 1-shot and 5-shot on miniImageNet → miniImageNet, Meta-ProtoNet achieves about 1% higher performance than Prototypical Network. However, Meta-ProtoNet achieves 5% and 10% higher performance for 1-shot and 5-shot on CUB → CUB, and 3% and 6% higher performance on SUN → SUN. As the latter two scenarios are conducted on fine-grained classification datasets, we attribute the promising improvement to that the categories in these fine-grained datasets share more local concepts than those in coarse-grained datasets, and thus a more discriminative space can be rapidly learned with a few steps of adaptation. Moreover, Meta-ProtoNet achieves the best performance among all baselines in all conventional FSL scenarios, which shows that our approach can be considered as a better baseline option under the conventional FSL setting.

Evaluation Using the Cross-Domain Setting. We also conduct cross-domain FSL experiments and report the comparative results in Table 2. Compared to the results under the conventional setting, it can be observed that all approaches suffer from a larger discrepancy between the distributions of training and testing tasks, which results in a performance decline in all scenarios. However, Meta-ProtoNet still outperforms the original Prototypical Network in all cross-domain FSL scenarios, demonstrating that the bilevel optimization strategy for adaptation and the learning of transferable latent factors can be utilized to improve simple metric-based approaches. Also, Meta-ProtoNet achieves all the best results, indicating that our approach can be regarded as a promising baseline under the cross-domain setting.

4 Conclusion

In this paper, we propose Meta-ProtoNet to handle the challenge of heterogeneous task distributions in few-shot scenarios, aiming to learn a latent factor space in which metric-based classification of heterogeneous tasks can be better performed. Extensive experiments show that our proposed approach can be considered as a stronger baseline in both conventional and cross-domain few-shot settings.

References

Xiaobin Chang, Yongxin Yang, Tao Xiang, and Timothy M Hospedales. 2019. Disjoint label space transfer learning with common factorised space. In *Proceedings of the AAAI Conference on Artificial Intelligence*, volume 33, pages 3288–3295.

Wei-Yu Chen, Yen-Cheng Liu, Zsolt Kira, Yu-Chiang Frank Wang, and Jia-Bin Huang. 2019. A closer look at few-shot classification. In *7th International Conference on Learning Representations, ICLR 2019, New Orleans, LA, USA, May 6-9, 2019.*

Chelsea Finn, Pieter Abbeel, and Sergey Levine. 2017. Model-agnostic meta-learning for fast adaptation of deep networks. In *Proceedings of the 34th International Conference on Machine Learning, ICML 2017, Sydney, NSW, Australia, 6-11 August 2017*, pages 1126–1135.

Diederik P Kingma and Jimmy Ba. 2014. Adam: A method for stochastic optimization. *arXiv preprint arXiv:1412.6980.*

Qi Li, Zhenan Sun, Ran He, and Tieniu Tan. 2017. Deep supervised discrete hashing. *arXiv preprint arXiv:1705.10999.*

Genevieve Patterson, Chen Xu, Hang Su, and James Hays. 2014. The sun attribute database: Beyond categories for deeper scene understanding. *International Journal of Computer Vision*, 108(1-2):59–81.

Jake Snell, Kevin Swersky, and Richard S. Zemel. 2017. Prototypical networks for few-shot learning. In *Advances in Neural Information Processing Systems 30: Annual Conference on Neural Information Processing Systems 2017, 4-9 December 2017, Long Beach, CA, USA*, pages 4077–4087.

Ashish Vaswani, Noam Shazeer, Niki Parmar, Jakob Uszkoreit, Llion Jones, Aidan N Gomez, Lukasz Kaiser, and Illia Polosukhin. 2017. Attention is all you need. *arXiv preprint arXiv:1706.03762.*

Oriol Vinyals, Charles Blundell, Timothy Lillicrap, Daan Wierstra, et al. 2016. Matching networks for one shot learning. In *NeurIPS*, pages 3630–3638.

Catherine Wah, Steve Branson, Peter Welinder, Pietro Perona, and Serge Belongie. 2011. The caltech-ucsd birds-200-2011 dataset.

Reference and coreference in situated dialogue

Sharid Loáiciga[1]   **Simon Dobnik**[2]   **David Schlangen**[1]
[1]Computational Linguistics, Department of Linguistics, University of Potsdam, Germany
[2]CLASP, Department of Philosophy, Linguistics and Theory of Science,
University of Gothenburg, Sweden
`{loaicigasanchez, david.schlangen}@uni-potsdam.de,`
`simon.dobnik@gu.se`

Abstract

In recent years, a large number of corpora have been developed for vision and language tasks. We argue that there is still significant room for corpora that increase the complexity of both visual and linguistic domains and which capture different varieties of perceptual and conversational contexts. Working with two corpora approaching this goal, we present a linguistic perspective on some of the challenges in creating and extending resources combining language and vision while preserving continuity with the existing best practices in the area of coreference annotation.

1 Introduction

With the ease of combining representations from different modalities provided by neural networks, text and vision are coming together. There is a growing body of resources addressing a setting in which the visual context can be exploited to support a textual task, for example visual coreference resolution.

Several corpora have been developed in the domain of vision and language (V&L), for example corpora of image captions (Lin et al., 2014; Young et al., 2014; Krishna et al., 2017), images and paragraph descriptions (Krause et al., 2017), visual question answering (Antol et al., 2015), visual dialogue (Das et al., 2017) and embodied question answering (Das et al., 2018). Through these the V&L research has progressively moved from sentence descriptions to descriptions involving utterances and conversations, therefore adding complexity to their semantic representations. In parallel to the corpora, V&L systems have been developed but of course these are limited by the complexity of the task for which the dataset has been collected. The end goal of the current research is to move to a more complex linguistic setting involving multiparty dialogue and visual representations that go beyond individual images.

Situated reference resolution involves grounding linguistic expressions in perceptual representations (Harnad, 1990). Coreference resolution, traditionally a textual task, involves linking linguistic expressions referring to the same discourse entities (Stede, 2012). While challenging, the task is defined by the familiar nature of written texts: linear, planned and structured; defining thus the coreference mechanisms and devices found in them. In resources combining V&L, however, the textual part is often a dialogue or pairs of question-answers. As a result, the coreference devices differ considerably from those found in texts and are closer to actual conversations whereby people create reference to entities on the fly. This of course comes with its own challenges, but there are also some relations made easier since they can be grounded in the image.

As V&L come together, there is therefore an increased need for extending resources for the task of visual coreference resolution. This means engaging with the challenges along two axes:

- Dialogue: built by two speakers who each have their own mental state and cognitive process but who are communicating through referring expressions which are projected in the same conversation.
- Shared physical context: simultaneous access to an image or other perceptual context which enables non-linear references to it. Instead, the reference is guided by visual attention.

We present a linguistic perspective on these challenges by analysing a pilot annotation of two situated dialogue corpora: the *Cups* corpus (Dobnik et al., 2020) and the *Tell-me-more* corpus (Ilinykh et al., 2019), shown below in Figure 1 and example (1) respectively. Starting from the annotation scheme for several textual coreference datasets (Artstein and Poesio, 2006; Pradhan et al., 2007; Uryupina et al., 2019), this exercise proved useful to pinpoint in what ways the purely textual doc-

Proceedings of the Second Workshop on Advances in Language and Vision Research, pages 39–44

ument scenario is different from the domain of embodied interaction.

The first corpus contains a conversation between two participants over an almost identical visual scene involving a table and cups where participants have different locations (Figure 1). Some cups have been removed from each participant's view and they are instructed to discuss over a computer terminal in order to find the cups that each does not see. The *Tell-me-more* corpus consists of images accompanied with a small text of five complete sentences, collected by asking participants to describe the image to a friend, successively adding details. The genre of these texts is therefore mixed: in between standard text (as found in news text for example) and dialogue data which reflects the features found in conversations rather than written conventions.

These corpora are complementary as *Cups* gives us accurate visual ground truth information with free and unrestricted dialogue, while *Tell-me-more* offers a richer unrestricted image with short and task constrained (pseudo-)dialogues.

In this paper, we discuss a number of cases from these corpora that challenge both standard language grounding annotations as well as standard coreference annotation. This work points thus towards required future work in creating (co)reference annotation schemes that can handle situated dialogue.

2 Related Work

Pointing to the inability of NLP tools to handle the textual part in situated dialogue, early works had described the need to ground the dialogue in the image in a manner informed by linguistics (Byron, 2003).

As content develops in a text, entities are introduced and re-mentioned, establishing discourse referents. The context is provided by the document and no extra-linguistic reference is needed for resolving the reference to an entity (Karttunen, 1969). In situated dialogue, on the other hand, the visual modality brings the extra-linguistic context as a source of referents. Here, resolving references to entities can be thus achieved by either looking at the picture or by reading the discourse. Recording both strategies separately is crucial if we want to understand and model them soundly, in keeping with theories of cognitive processing (cf. (Kelleher et al., 2005)). Extending the coreference annotation paradigm is thus the best bet although not a lot

(a) Perspective of participant 1.

(b) Perspective of participant 2.

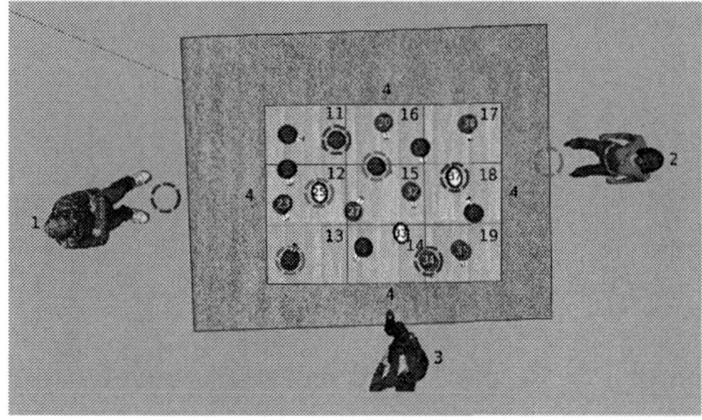

(c) Top-down perspective of the Cups corpus scene with ground truth object IDs.

Figure 1: Participant 1 cannot see the cups circled in blue, whereas participant 2 cannot see the cups circled in red. Person 3 is visible to both participants as a reference point.

of work exists in this area.

Textual coreference Annotated data for the coreference resolution task has mainly focused on news texts and concrete nouns, excluding reference to events and other coreferential relations such as bridging, deixis, and ambiguous items well documented in the linguistic literature but deemed infrequent or too difficult to process (Poesio, 2016). In contrast, there is a growing body of literature interested in phenomena beyond the nominal case (Kolhatkar et al., 2018; Nedoluzhko and Lapshinova-Koltunski, 2016), resulting in new, although still small in size, annotated corpora (Lapshinova-Koltunski et al., 2018; Zeldes, 2017; Uryupina et al., 2020).

Visual coreference Coreference work based on the popular VisDial dataset (Das et al., 2017) targets only a limited set of referential expressions, partly because it relies on automatic tools (Kottur et al., 2018; Yu et al., 2019), which are known to be problematic with this genre. With a focus in grounded human interaction, there are corpora whose textual part comprises question answer pairs (Antol et al., 2015; Goyal et al., 2017). Those, however, are short in nature, with few opportunities for re-mention of the different objects in the image and hence coreference. Last, corpora designed towards navigation and location (Stoia et al., 2008; Thomason et al., 2019) focusing on different kind of task and descriptions might be good candidates that could be explored and extended in a similar fashion as our corpora.

Referring expressions generation The goal in this area is to generate expressions over several turns of conversation in a natural and non-repetitive way, following principles of communicative discourse as for example in the recent PhotoBook dataset (Takmaz et al., 2020). Our work is complementary to such undertakings as it focuses on the interpretative rather than generative part.

3 Understanding reference in situated dialogue

The notion of coreference chain–the sequence of mentions pointing to a same entity in a text–is central in coreference resolution. Built on top of the document as a unit, this notion relies on and in turn informs theories about accessibility hierarchy and salience of entities (Ariel, 1988, 2004; Grosz et al., 1995). In dialogue, however, references crisscross between the speakers and, one step further, in situated dialogue references crisscross between the speakers and the objects in the image. In this section we revise the annotation challenges in the annotation of anaphoric phenomena in data of this genre.

3.1 Grounding and referentiality

In spoken discourse people try their best to ground the references so they make sure they understand each other. To do so, they rely on the mechanisms of attention (Lavie et al., 2004). Although most concrete references can be grounded to the image easily, there are also some difficult cases. References can be found to portions of the image without a bounding box, such as *base of the tub* in example (1).

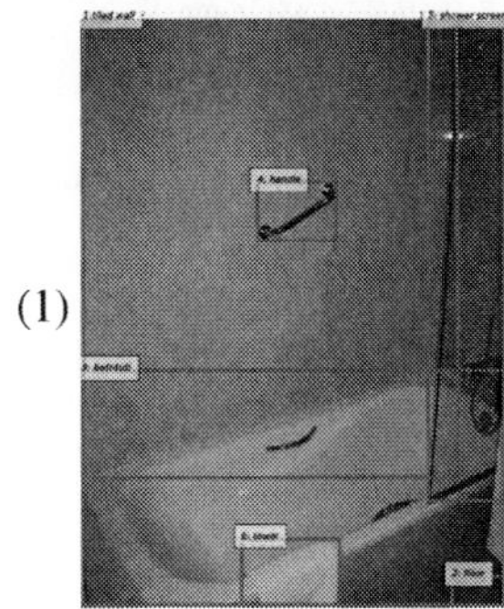

(1)
```
1.  This is a
picture of a
bathtub.
2.  The tub is
white.
3.  The wall
and base of the
tub are brown.
4.  The door
appears to be
glass.
5.  There is a
handrail on the
side wall.
```

In the previous example the difficulty arises because the object detector failed to recognise the target object. However, referring expressions are referential to a different degree, e.g., "Where are your blue ones?" – is the speaker referring to a particular subset of blue cups, all the blue cups in the scene, blue cups in general, or not referring to any particular set of objects? The distinction is sometimes not clear.

Last, as the image determines the scope of the referentiality, typical semantic properties are frequently used to refer back to the objects in the image: colour, shapes, sizes. These can be genuinely referential (a form of ellipsis) or used in an attributive manner. Compare for example *white* in the second sentence of (1), with (2) below.

(2)
```
P1:  closest to me, from left to
right red, blue, white, red
P2:  ok, on your side I only see
red, blue, white
```

3.2 Speakers' cognitive state

Contrary to a Gricean-based analysis of spoken discourse, coherence-based theories of discourse do not traditionally take the cognitive state of the speaker as a necessary element to text interpretation (Bender and Lascarides, 2019). In situated dialogue, however, although the image can be treated as the ground truth of the situation, the speaker's cognitive state has to be considered to disambiguate their utterances, the hearer makes a model of their beliefs, desires and intentions associated with the utterance. This is exemplified in the following excerpt from *Cups* where both participants do not see one of the two red cups close by, but each a different one. They mistakenly believe that there is only one missing red cup and this dis-alignment of their beliefs gradually leads to increasingly diverging cognitive states.

(3)
```
P2: there is an empty space on
the table on the second row away
from you
P2: between the red and white mug
(from left to right)
P1: I have one thing there, a
white funny top
P2: ok, i'll mark it.
DIALOGUE_STATE: B found O-25.
P1: and the red one is slightly
close to you
P1: is that right?
P1: to my left from that red mug
there is a yellow mug
P2: hm...
P2: can't see that and now i'm
confused
DIALOGUE_STATE: B cannot see O-29.
P2: describe the second row away
from you like you see it
P1: only one thing there, a white
funny top
P2: aha, so it's closer to you
than those i call "the second row"
P1: behind that, there is a
yellow, red, white and blue
P1: from my left to right
P1: yes, that must be it!
P1: so what do you see in the
"second row" from my perspective?
P2: i see a red, then space, then
white and blue (same as katie's")
P2: no yellow
P2: is it on the edge of the
table?
P2: on your left
P1: ok, yes!
DIALOGUE_STATE: inconsistent
```

3.3 Level of specification

We observe a common strategy of grouping things in order to refer to them collectively. This raises the question: What is the level of specification needed in a coreference annotation? One could think about this in linguistic terms, for instance mass nouns or sets; alternatively, in computer vision, there is the distinction between things and stuff (Caesar et al., 2018).

In (4) below, is the reference to the *curtains* a case of a set composed by individual instances, or is it a mass noun? Note the curtains is a type of stuff in Caesar et al.'s work.

(4)
```
1. I see a picture of an
entertainment room. 2. there
is a round table in the foreground
and a fussball table in the middle
of the room, as well as a pool
table further back. 3. there is
a sitting area with chairs facing
a television set. 4. the room
has several windows with green
curtains. 5.the floors are made
of a brown tile.
```

In (5) from Cups, on the other hand, the speakers refer to *rows* of objects even though these are not arranged in strict geometric lines. Hence, which objects are included is contextually defined and not always clear.

(5)
```
P2: ok, so your next row
P2: you said there 's a takeaway
cup somewhere marooned all alone
P1: Okay. So we have that row I
described with the now found red
cup. Then a takeaway cup that
is between that row and the next.
It's very much in the middle of
the two rows.
```

3.4 Information status

Different referring expressions have different properties and behaviour, an idea behind theories of salience and accessibility. They are based on the observation that some forms are used to introduce entities and some others to refer to them: some entities are discourse-new and some are discourse-old. In situated dialogue, the image provides an additional context and source of referents, but it does not follow that the status of subsequent mentions is *old*. In the example below, the fact that the discourse starts with *It* is licensed by the image and this source of reference should be accounted for differently in the annotation than a genuine discourse-old case such as the *it* in sentence 2.

```
(6)    1.  It s a well-lit kitchen with
       stainded [sic] wooden cupboards .
       2.  There's a microwave mounted
       over the stove, which has a
       red tea kettle on it.  3.  The
       appliances are black and stainless
       steel in the kitchen.  4.  The
       countertops look like they 're
       black granite.  5.  The window has
       sunlight streaming in and it 's
       very brightly light.
```

4 Conclusions

V&L resources provide a unique opportunity to explore the notion of discourse entity in grounded context. Extending the coreference annotation to this domain is essential to understand the relationship between reference and coreference. The same mechanisms that humans adopt to solve coreference in the textual domain should underlay results in the V&L domain. Indeed, reference is underspecified in both modalities; any kind of information extraction from these domains will benefit from mechanisms that resolve this underspecification: capturing coreference is a door to capturing coherence. Furthermore, a rich annotation scheme leads to the development of corpora allowing the training of data driven systems for the V&L domain and social robotics.

References

Stanislaw Antol, Aishwarya Agrawal, Jiasen Lu, Margaret Mitchell, Dhruv Batra, C. Lawrence Zitnick, and Devi Parikh. 2015. VQA: Visual Question Answering. In *Proceedings of the IEEE International Conference on Computer Vision (ICCV)*.

Mira Ariel. 1988. Referring and accessibility. *Journal of Linguistics*, 24(1):65–87.

Mira Ariel. 2004. Accessibility marking: Discourse functions, discourse profiles, and processing cues. *Discourse Processes*, 37(2):91–116.

Ron Artstein and Massimo Poesio. 2006. Arrau annotation manual (trains dialogues).

Emily M. Bender and Alex Lascarides. 2019. Linguistic Fundamentals for Natural Language Processing II: 100 Essentials from Semantics and Pragmatics. *Synthesis Lectures on Human Language Technologies*, 12(3):1–268.

Donna K Byron. 2003. Understanding referring expressions in situated language some challenges for real-world agents. In *Proceedings of the First International Workshop on Language Understanding and Agents for Real World Interaction*, pages 39–47.

Holger Caesar, Jasper Uijlings, and Vittorio Ferrari. 2018. Coco-stuff: Thing and stuff classes in context. In *Proceedings of the IEEE Conference on Computer Vision and Pattern Recognition (CVPR)*.

Abhishek Das, Samyak Datta, Georgia Gkioxari, Stefan Lee, Devi Parikh, and Dhruv Batra. 2018. Embodied question answering. In *Proceedings of the IEEE Conference on Computer Vision and Pattern Recognition Workshops*, pages 2054–2063.

Abhishek Das, Satwik Kottur, Khushi Gupta, Avi Singh, Deshraj Yadav, José MF Moura, Devi Parikh, and Dhruv Batra. 2017. Visual dialog. In *Proceedings of the IEEE Conference on Computer Vision and Pattern Recognition*, pages 326–335.

Simon Dobnik, John D. Kelleher, and Christine Howes. 2020. Local alignment of frame of reference assignment in English and Swedish dialogue. In *Spatial Cognition XII: Proceedings of the 12th International Conference, Spatial Cognition 2020, Riga, Latvia*, pages 251–267, Cham, Switzerland. Springer International Publishing.

Yash Goyal, Tejas Khot, Douglas Summers-Stay, Dhruv Batra, and Devi Parikh. 2017. Making the V in VQA matter: Elevating the role of image understanding in Visual Question Answering. In *Conference on Computer Vision and Pattern Recognition (CVPR)*.

Barbara J. Grosz, Aravind K. Joshi, and Scott Weinstein. 1995. Centering: A framework for modelling the local coherence of discourse. *Computational Linguistics*, 2(21):203–225.

Stevan Harnad. 1990. The symbol grounding problem. *Physica D*, 42(1–3):335–346.

Nikolai Ilinykh, Sina Zarrieß, and David Schlangen. 2019. Tell me more: A dataset of visual scene description sequences. In *Proceedings of the 12th International Conference on Natural Language Generation*, pages 152–157, Tokyo, Japan. Association for Computational Linguistics.

Lauri Karttunen. 1969. Discourse referents. In *International Conference on Computational Linguistics COLING 1969: Preprint No. 70*, Sånga Säby, Sweden.

John D. Kelleher, Fintan J. Costello, and Josef van Genabith. 2005. Dynamically structuring updating and interrelating representations of visual and linguistic discourse. *Artificial Intelligence*, 167:62–102.

Varada Kolhatkar, Adam Roussel, Stefanie Dipper, and Heike Zinsmeister. 2018. Anaphora with nonnominal antecedents in computational linguistics: a survey. *Computational Linguistics*, 44(3):547–612.

Satwik Kottur, José M. F. Moura, Devi Parikh, Dhruv Batra, and Marcus Rohrbach. 2018. Visual coreference resolution in visual dialog using neural module networks. In *The European Conference on Computer Vision (ECCV)*.

Jonathan Krause, Justin Johnson, Ranjay Krishna, and Li Fei-Fei. 2017. A hierarchical approach for generating descriptive image paragraphs. In *2017 IEEE Conference on Computer Vision and Pattern Recognition (CVPR)*, pages 3337–3345.

Ranjay Krishna, Yuke Zhu, Oliver Groth, Justin Johnson, Kenji Hata, Joshua Kravitz, Stephanie Chen, Yannis Kalantidis, Li-Jia Li, David A Shamma, Michael Bernstein, and Li Fei-Fei. 2017. Visual Genome: Connecting language and vision using crowdsourced dense image annotations. *International Journal of Computer Vision*, 123(1):32–73.

Ekaterina Lapshinova-Koltunski, Christian Hardmeier, and Pauline Krielke. 2018. ParCorFull: a parallel corpus annotated with full coreference. In *Proceedings of 11th Language Resources and Evaluation Conference*, pages 423–428, Miyazaki, Japan. European Language Resources Association (ELRA). To appear.

Nilli Lavie, Aleksandra Hirst, Jan W de Fockert, and Essi Viding. 2004. Load theory of selective attention and cognitive control. *Journal of Experimental Psychology: General*, 133(3):339–354.

Tsung-Yi Lin, Michael Maire, Serge Belongie, James Hays, Pietro Perona, Deva Ramanan, Piotr Dollár, and C. Lawrence Zitnick. 2014. Microsoft coco: Common objects in context. In *Computer Vision – ECCV 2014*, pages 740–755, Cham. Springer International Publishing.

Anna Nedoluzhko and Ekaterina Lapshinova-Koltunski. 2016. Abstract coreference in a multilingual perspective: a view on czech and german. In *Proceedings of the Workshop on Coreference Resolution Beyond OntoNotes*, CORBON 2016, pages 47–52, Ann Arbor, Michigan. Association for Computational Linguistics.

Massimo Poesio. 2016. Linguistic and cognitive evidence about anaphora. In Massimo Poesio, Roland Stuckardt, and Yannick Versley, editors, *Anaphora Resolution: Algorithms, Resources and Applications*, pages 23–54. Springer-Verlag, Berlin Heidelberg.

Sameer S. Pradhan, Lance Ramshaw, Ralph Weischedel, and Jessica MacBrideand Linnea Micciulla. 2007. Unrestricted coreference: Identifying entities and events in OntoNotes. In *International Conference on Semantic Computing (ICSC 2007)*, pages 446–453.

Manfred Stede. 2012. *Disourse Processing*. Morgan and Claypool Publishers, Toronto.

Laura Stoia, Darla Magdalene Shockley, Donna K. Byron, and Eric Fosler-Lussier. 2008. SCARE: a situated corpus with annotated referring expressions. In *Proceedings of the Sixth International Conference on Language Resources and Evaluation (LREC'08)*, Marrakech, Morocco. European Language Resources Association (ELRA).

Ece Takmaz, Mario Giulianelli, Sandro Pezzelle, Arabella Sinclair, and Raquel Fernández. 2020. Refer, Reuse, Reduce: Generating Subsequent References in Visual and Conversational Contexts. In *Proceedings of the 2020 Conference on Empirical Methods in Natural Language Processing (EMNLP)*, pages 4350–4368, Online. Association for Computational Linguistics.

Jesse Thomason, Michael Murray, Maya Cakmak, and Luke Zettlemoyer. 2019. Vision-and-dialog navigation. In *Conference on Robot Learning (CoRL)*.

Olga Uryupina, Ron Artstein, Antonella Bristot, Federica Cavicchio, Francesca Delogu, Kepa Rodriguez, and Massimo Poesio. 2020. Annotating a broad range of anaphoric phenomena, in multiple genres: the ARRAU corpus. *Natural Language Engineering*, 26(1):95–128.

Olga Uryupina, Ron Artstein, Antonella Bristot, Federica Cavicchio, Francesca Delogu, Kepa J. Rodriguez, and Massimo Poesio. 2019. Annotating a broad range of anaphoric phenomena, in a variety of genres: the ARRAU corpus. *Natural Language Engineering*, 26(1):95–128.

Peter Young, Alice Lai, Micah Hodosh, and Julia Hockenmaier. 2014. From image descriptions to visual denotations: New similarity metrics for semantic inference over event descriptions. *Transactions of the Association for Computational Linguistics*, 2:67–78.

Xintong Yu, Hongming Zhang, Yangqiu Song, Yan Song, and Changshui Zhang. 2019. What you see is what you get: Visual pronoun coreference resolution in dialogues. In *Proceedings of the 2019 Conference on Empirical Methods in Natural Language Processing and the 9th International Joint Conference on Natural Language Processing (EMNLP-IJCNLP)*, pages 5123–5132, Hong Kong, China. Association for Computational Linguistics.

Amir Zeldes. 2017. The GUM corpus: creating multilayer resources in the classroom. *Language Resources and Evaluation*, 51(3):581–612.

Language-based Video Editing via Multi-Modal Multi-Level Transformer

Tsu-Jui Fu[†], Xin Eric Wang[‡], Scott T. Grafton[†], Miguel P. Eckstein[†], William Yang Wang[†]

[†]UC Santa Barbara   [‡]UC Santa Cruz
{tsu-juifu, william}@cs.ucsb.edu, xwang366@ucsc.edu
{scott.grafton, miguel.eckstein}@psych.ucsb.edu

Abstract

Video editing tools are widely used nowadays for digital design. Although the demand for these tools is high, the prior knowledge required makes it difficult for novices to get started. Systems that could follow natural language instructions to perform automatic editing would significantly improve accessibility. This paper introduces the language-based video editing (LBVE) task, which allows the model to edit, guided by text instruction, a source video into a target video. LBVE contains two features: 1) the scenario of the source video is preserved instead of generating a completely different video; 2) the semantic is presented differently in the target video, and all changes are controlled by the given instruction. We propose a Multi-Modal Multi-Level Transformer (M^3L-Transformer) to carry out LBVE. The M^3L-Transformer dynamically learns the correspondence between video perception and language semantic at different levels, which benefits both the video understanding and video frame synthesis. We build three new datasets for evaluation, including two diagnostic and one from natural videos with human-labeled text. Extensive experimental results show that M^3L-Transformer is effective for video editing and that LBVE can lead to a new field toward vision-and-language research.

1. Introduction

Video is one of the most direct ways to convey information, as people are used to interacting with this world via dynamic visual perception. Nowadays, video editing tools like Premiere and Final Cut are widely applied for digital design usages, such as film editing or video effects. However, those applications require prior knowledge and complex operations to utilize successfully, which makes it difficult for novices to get started. For humans, natural language is the most natural way of communication. If a system can follow the given language instructions and automatically perform

Project site: https://lbvce2515.github.io/

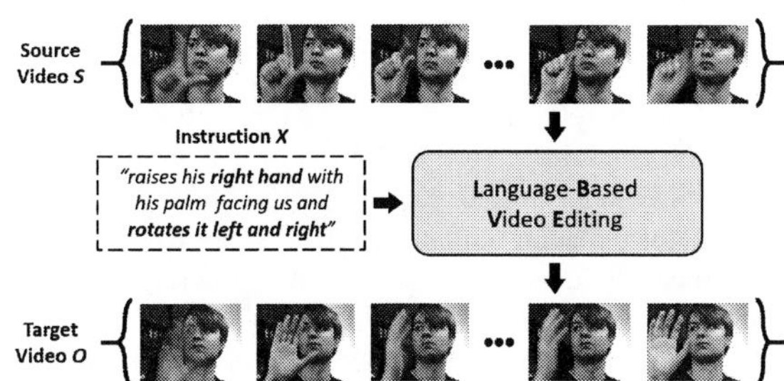

Figure 1. The introduced language-based video editing (LBVE) task. LBVE requires to edit a source video S into the target video T guided by the instruction X.

related editing actions, it will significantly improve accessibility and meet the considerable demand.

In this paper, we introduce language-based video editing (LBVE), a general V2V task, where the target video is controllable directly by language instruction. LBVE treats a video and an instruction as the input, and the target video is edited from the textual description. As illustrated in Fig. 1, the same person performs different hand gestures guided by the instruction. Different from text-to-video (T2V) [33, 3, 44, 39], video editing enjoys two following feature: 1) the scenario (e.g., scene or humans) of the source video is preserved instead of generating all content from scratch; 2) the semantic (e.g., property of the object or moving action) is presented differently in the target video. The main challenge of LBVE is to link the video perception with language understanding and reflect what semantics should be manipulated during the video generation but under a similar scenario. People usually take further editing steps onto a base video rather than create all content from the beginning. We believe that our LBVE is more practical and corresponding to human daily usage.

To tackle the LBVE task, we propose a multi-modal multi-level transformer (M^3L) to perform video editing conditioning on the guided text. As shown in Fig. 2, M^3L contains a multi-modal multi-level Transformer where the encoder models the moving motion to understand the entire

Proceedings of the Second Workshop on Advances in Language and Vision Research, pages 45–56
©2021 Association for Computational Linguistics

video, and the decoder serves as a global planner to generate each frame of the target video. For better video perception to link with the given instruction, the incorporated multi-level fusion fuses between these two modalities. During encoding, the local-level fusion is applied with the text tokens for fine-grained visual understanding, and the global-level fusion extracts the key feature of the moving motion. Reversely, during decoding, we first adopt global-level fusion from whole instruction to give a high-level plan for the target video, and then the local-level fusion can further generate each frame in detail with the specific property. With multi-level fusion, M^3L learns explicit vision-and-language perception between the video and given instruction, yielding better video synthesis.

For evaluation, we collect three datasets under the brand-new LBVE task. There are E-MNIST and E-CLEVR, where we build from hand-written number recognition MNIST [31] and compositional VQA CLEVR [26], respectively. Both E-MNIST and E-CLEVR are prepared for evaluating the content replacing (different numbers or shapes and colors) and semantic manipulation (different moving directions or related positions). To investigate the capability of LBVE for natural video with open text, E-JESTER is built upon the same person performing different hand gestures with human-labeled instruction.

Our experimental results show that the multi-modal multi-level transformer (M^3L) can carry out the LBVE task, and the multi-level fusion further helps between video perception and language understanding in both aspects of content replacing and semantic manipulation. In summary, our contributions are four-fold:

- We introduce the LBVE task to manipulate video content controlled by text instructions.
- We present M^3L to perform LBVE, where the multi-level fusion further helps between video perception and language understanding.
- For evaluation under LBVE, we prepare three new datasets containing two diagnostic and one natural video with human-labeled text.
- Extensive ablation studies show that our M^3L is adequate for video editing, and LBVE can lead to a new field toward vision-and-language research.

2. Related Work

Language-based Image Editing Different from text-to-image (T2I) [43, 48, 55], which generates an image that matches the given instruction, language-based image editing (LBIE) understands the visual difference and edits between two images based on the guided text description. Image Spirit [10] and PixelTone [30] first propose the LBIE framework but accept only rule-based instruction and pre-defined semantic labels, which limits the practi-cality of LBIE. Inspired by numerous GAN-based methods [47, 74, 71] in T2I, there are some previous works [9, 52] perform LBIE as image colorization by the conditional GAN. Since humans do not always finish editing all-at-once but will involve several different steps, iterative LBIE (ILBIE) [14, 15] is proposed to imitate the actual process by the multi-turn manipulation and modeling the instructed editing history. Similar to LBIE, language-based video editing (LBVE) is to edit the content in a video by the guided instruction. To perform LBVE, it is required to model the dynamic visual perception instead of just a still image and consider the temporal consistency of each frame during the generation to make a smooth result video.

Language-based Video Generation Generative video modeling [59, 4, 3, 45, 38, 53, 27, 66, 2, 13, 22, 50, 49, 60, 41, 56, 11, 23, 18, 19, 39] is a widely-discussed research topic that looks into the capability of a model to generate a video purely in pixel space. Built upon video generation, text-to-video (T2V) [33, 3, 44, 39] synthesizes a video by the guided text description, which makes the video output controllable by the natural language. In this paper, we investigate the video editing task, which replaces the specific object with different properties or changes the moving motion in the input video. Different from generating video from scratch, video editing requires extracting the dynamic visual perception of the source video and manipulating the semantic inside to generate the target video.

Video-to-Video Synthesis Video super-resolution [25, 1, 34, 36], segmentation video reconstruction [63, 62], video style transfer [8, 67, 12], or video inpainting [6, 28, 70] can be considered as the particular case of video-to-video synthesis (V2V). Since they all depend on the task themselves, the variability between source-target is still under the problem-specific constraint. Among them, video prediction [46, 61, 32, 17], which predicts future frames conditioning on the given video, is one of the most related to our present LBVE task. Both video prediction and LBVE should understand the hidden semantic of the given video first and then predict the target frames with different content inside. While for video prediction, there are many possibilities of appeared future events, which makes it not deterministic for real-world usage [39]. On the other hand, LBVE is controllable by the given instruction, which involves both content replacing (object changing) and semantic manipulation (moving action changing). With the guided text description, LBVE can perform V2V with content editing and lead to predictable target video.

3. Language-based Video Editing

3.1. Task Definition

We study the language-based video editing (LBVE) task to edit a source video S into a target video O by a given

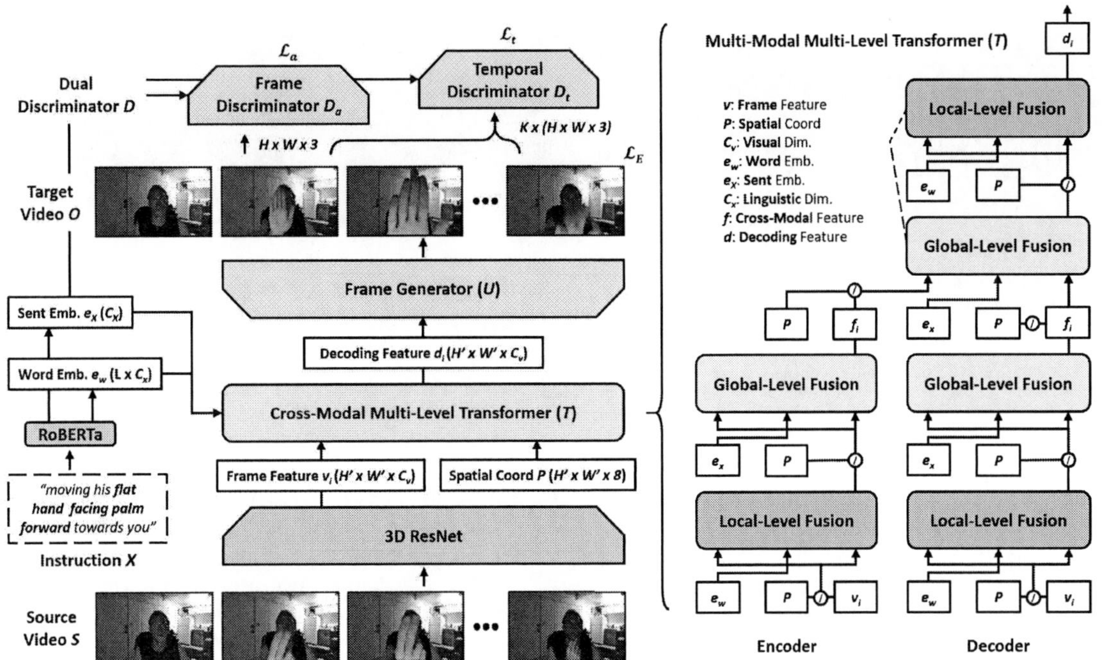

Figure 2. An overview architecture of our multi-modal multi-level transformer (M^3L). M^3L contains the multi-modal multi-level transformer T to encode the source video S and decode for the target video frame o by the multi-level fusion (MLF).

instruction X, as shown in Fig. 1. Specifically, the source video S contains N frames as $\{s_1, s_2, ..., s_N\}$, and the instruction $X = \{w_1, w_2, ..., w_L\}$ where L is the number of word token in X. The target video O also includes N frames as $\{o_1, o_2, ..., o_N\}$. For LBVE, the model should preserve the scenario from S but change the related semantics in O guided by X. Note that the editing process is at a pixel level where the model has to generate each pixel of each frame and then assemble them as the target video.

3.2. Overview

An overview of our multi-modal multi-level transformer (M^3L) for LBVE is illustrated in Fig. 2. M^3L first extracts the frame feature v_i for the frame s_i in the source video S; the sentence embedding e_X and each word embedding e_w for the instruction X. Then, the multi-modal multi-level transformer T is proposed to model the sequential information of the source and the target video as the decoding feature d_i. In particular, the multi-level fusion (MLF) performs the cross-modal fusion between video v and instruction $\{e_X, e_w\}$. The local-level fusion (LF) extracts which portion is perceived by token e_w across all words in X. Besides, the global-level fusion (GF) models the interaction between the entire video perception and the semantic motion from the whole instruction e_X. Finally, with d_i, the generator U generates the frame o_i in the target video O. In addition, we apply the dual discriminator D, where

the frame discriminator D_a helps the quality of every single frame, and the temporal discriminator D_t maintains the consistency as a smooth output video.

Frame and Linguistic Feature Extraction To perform the LBVE task, We first apply a 3D ResNet and RoBERTa language model [37] to extract the frame feature v and linguistic feature $\{e_X, e_w\}$ for the two modalities independently:

$$\{v_1, v_2, ..., v_N\} = \text{3D ResNet}(\{s_1, s_2, ..., s_N\}),$$
$$e_X, \{e_{w_1}, e_{w_2}, ..., e_{w_L}\} = \text{RoBERTa}(X), \quad (1)$$

where e_{w_i} is the word embedding of each token w_i, e_X is the entire sentence embedding of X, and L represents the length of the instruction X. In detail, $v \in \mathbb{R}^{H' \times W' \times C_v}$ and each $e \in \mathbb{R}^{C_x}$, where C_v and C_x is the feature dimension of vision and language, respectively.

3.3. Multi-Modal Multi-Level Transformer

As illustrated in Fig. 2, with the frame feature v and linguistic feature $\{e_X, e_w\}$ as the inputs, the multi-modal multi-level transformer T contains an encoder to model the sequential information of the source video S with the given instruction X, and a decoder to acquire the decoding feature d_i for generating the target video frame o_i. Both the encoder and decoder are composed of multi-level fusion (MLF), which is applied to fuse between vision and language with aspects from different levels.

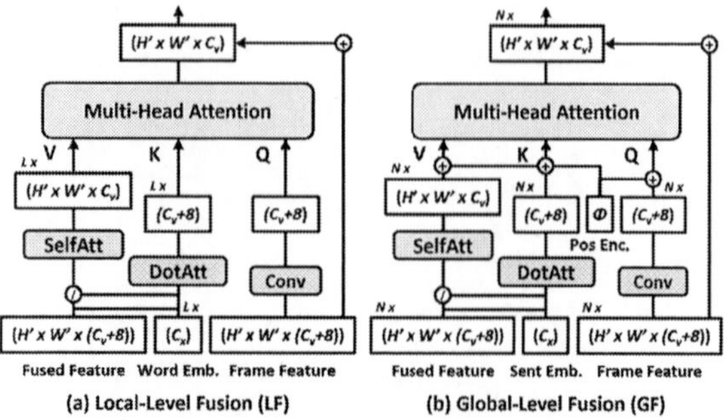

Figure 3. The computing flow of the multi-level fusion (MLF). The local-level fusion (LF) and the global-level fusion (GF)

Multi-Level Fusion Both video and language are multi-level conveyed, where video is composed of a series of image frames and language is a set of word tokens with a specific order. The multi-level fusion (MLF) consists of the local-level fusion (LF) to fuse between a single frame and each word token, and the global-level fusion (GF) models the entire video sequence with the whole instruction. The computation flow of MLF is illustrated in Fig. 3. Both LF and GF are computed with the multi-head attention (MHA) [58]. MHA acquires the weighted-sum of the value feature (V) by considering the correlation between the query feature (Q) and the key feature (K):

$$\mathrm{MHA}(\mathrm{Q},\mathrm{K},\mathrm{V}) = \mathrm{softmax}(\frac{\mathrm{Q}\cdot\mathrm{K}^T}{\sqrt{C_\mathrm{K}}})\mathrm{V}. \qquad (2)$$

For the local-level fusion (LF), it investigates which portion should be focused by each word e_w in a single frame v_i. We provide the relative spatial information by concatenating a 8-D spatial coordinate feature P [35] with v_i as p^L. To fuse between vision and language, we apply the self-attention mechanism (SelfAtt) [73, 72] upon the concatenated feature q^L to capture the correlation between word expression and visual context into s^L. Different from CMSA [72], which concatenates frame feature with all token embedding directly, our LF further considers the importance of each token. We adopt a 1-layer convolutional net (Conv) to extract the context-only visual feature c^L along the channel of v_i; and the widely-used dot-product attention (DotAtt) [69, 7] for the word-focused visual feature d_l^L with each word e_{w_l}. Therefore, the correlation between c^L and d_l^L can be considered as the important portion of word w_l for our LF. We treat the context-only visual feature c^L as K, the word-focused visual feature d_l^L as Q, and the cross-modal feature s^L as V to perform LF through MHA. We also utilize the residual connection [20, 58] in LF:

$$\mathrm{LF}(v_i^\mathrm{L}) = v_i^\mathrm{L} \oplus \mathrm{MHA}(\mathrm{c}^\mathrm{L}, \mathrm{d}^\mathrm{L}, \mathrm{s}^\mathrm{L}), \qquad (3)$$

where

$$\mathrm{p}^\mathrm{L} = [v_i^\mathrm{L}, P], \mathrm{q}^\mathrm{L} = \{[v_i^\mathrm{L}, P, e_{w_1}], ..., [v_i^\mathrm{L}, P, e_{w_L}]\},$$

$$\mathrm{c}^\mathrm{L} = \mathrm{Conv}^\mathrm{L}(\mathrm{p}^\mathrm{L}),$$

$$\mathrm{d}_l^\mathrm{L} = \mathrm{DotAtt}(\mathrm{p}^\mathrm{L}, e_{w_l}) = \sum_{(h,w)} \mathrm{softmax}(\mathrm{p}^\mathrm{L}\cdot W_\mathrm{d}^\mathrm{L}\cdot e_{w_l}^T)_{(h,w)}\cdot \mathrm{p}_{(h,w)}^\mathrm{L},$$

$$\mathrm{s}_l^\mathrm{L} = \mathrm{SelfAtt}(\mathrm{q}_l^\mathrm{L}), \mathrm{s}_{l(h,w)}^\mathrm{L} = \sum_{(x,y)} \mathrm{softmax}(\mathrm{q}_l^\mathrm{L}\cdot \mathrm{q}_{l(h,w)}^{\mathrm{L}\ T})_{(x,y)}\cdot \mathrm{q}_{l(x,y)}^\mathrm{L},$$

and W_d^L is the learnable attention matrix between p^L and e_w. In this way, our LF fuses between visual context and word expression from SelfAtt and take the important portion of each token from DotAtt into consideration.

For the global-level fusion (GF), it views the entire frame sequence $\{v_1, ..., v_N\}$ with the whole instruction e_X to extract the global motion of the video. Similar to LF, we acquire the fused cross-modal feature s_n^G from SelfAtt, the context-only visual feature c_n^G from Conv^G, and the sentence-focused visual feature d_n^G from DotAtt for v_n^G. To model the entire video, we follow [58], where the video-level feature of v_i can be represented as the relative weighted-sum over all frame-level v, and add on the positional encoding ϕ to incorporate the sequential order. We treat $\{\mathrm{s}_n^\mathrm{G}\}$ as V, $\{\mathrm{c}_n^\mathrm{G}\}$ as Q and $\{\mathrm{d}_n^\mathrm{G}\}$ as K for the correlation between a frame pair, to perform GF through MHA:

$$\mathrm{GF}(v^\mathrm{G}) = v^\mathrm{G} \oplus \mathrm{MHA}(\mathrm{c}^\mathrm{G}\oplus\phi, \mathrm{d}^\mathrm{G}\oplus\phi, \mathrm{s}^\mathrm{G}\oplus\phi), \qquad (4)$$

where

$$\mathrm{p}^\mathrm{G} = \{[v_1^\mathrm{G}, P], ..., [v_N^\mathrm{G}, P]\}, \quad \mathrm{q}^\mathrm{L} = \{[v_1^\mathrm{G}, P, e_X], ..., [v_N^\mathrm{G}, P, e_X]\},$$

$$\mathrm{c}_n^\mathrm{G} = \mathrm{Conv}^\mathrm{G}(\mathrm{p}^\mathrm{G})_n, \ \mathrm{d}_n^\mathrm{G} = \mathrm{DotAtt}(\mathrm{p}_n^\mathrm{G}, e_X), \ \mathrm{s}_n^\mathrm{G} = \mathrm{SelfAtt}(\mathrm{q}_n^\mathrm{G}).$$

By considering the correlation between frame with respect to the whole instruction from DotAtt, our GF models the video sequence as fused cross-modal feature from SelfAtt.

Encoder and Decoder The encoder (Enc) in the multi-modal multi-level transformer T serves to model the source video sequence S with the given instruction X. Enc first adopts the local-level fusion (LF) to extract important portion from each single frame v^s with each word embedding e_w; then the global-level fusion (GF) extracts the entire video motion with the sentence embedding e_X as the cross-modal feature f_i^s:

$$f_i^s = \mathrm{GF}(\mathrm{LF}(v^s, e_w), e_X)_i. \qquad (5)$$

During decoding, the decoder (Dec) also extracts the cross-modal feature f_i^o as the same way from the previous generated frames $\{o_1, ..., o_{i-1}\}$. To acquire the decoding feature d_i to generate the target frame, GF is first adopted to give the high-level concept of moving motion by the interaction between the cross-modal feature f from source and target, where we treat f^s as the fused feature (V). Then, LF is applied for detailed specific property provided from word tokens e_w:

$$f_i^o = \text{LF}(\text{GF}(\{v_1^o, ..., v_{i-1}^o\}, e_X|f^s)_i, e_w). \qquad (6)$$

In summary, the multi-modal multi-level transformer T models the source video frame v^s and the given instruction $\{e_X, e_w\}$, and considers previous generated target frames $\{o_1, ..., o_{i-1}\}$ to acquire the decoding feature d_i:

$$d_i = T(\{o_1, ..., o_{i-1}\}|v^s, \{e_X, e_w\}). \qquad (7)$$

3.4. Video Frame Generation

With the decoding feature d_i from T, we adopt Res-Blocks [42] into the generator U to scale up d_i and synthesize into $\hat{o}_i$:

$$\hat{o}_i = U(d_i), \qquad \hat{O} = \{\hat{o}_1, \hat{o}_2, ..., \hat{o}_N\}. \qquad (8)$$

We calculate the editing loss $\mathcal{L}_E$ as the average pixel difference using mean-square loss across each frame between O and $\hat{O}$:

$$\mathcal{L}_E = \frac{1}{N}\sum_{i=1}^{N}\text{MSELoss}(o_i, \hat{o}_i). \qquad (9)$$

Dual Discriminator Apart from the visual difference, we also consider the video quality of our generated $\hat{O}$. Similar to DVD-GAN [11], we apply the dual discriminator D, where the frame discriminator D_a improves the single frame quality and the temporal discriminator D_t constrains the temporal consistency for a smooth output video $\hat{O}$. We treat D_a as a binary classifier, which discriminates a target video frame o is from ground-truth O or our synthesized $\hat{O}$. Simultaneously, D_t judges that if K consecutive frames are smooth and consistent enough to be a real video fragment as the binary discrimination. The video quality loss $\mathcal{L}_G$ is computed for both frame quality and temporal consistency:

$$\mathcal{L}_{\hat{a}} = \frac{1}{N}\sum_{i=1}^{N}\log(1 - D_a(\hat{o}_i)),$$

$$\mathcal{L}_{\hat{t}} = \frac{1}{M}\sum_{i=1}^{M}\log(1 - D_t(\{\hat{o}_i, ..., \hat{o}_{i+K-1}\})), \qquad (10)$$

$$\mathcal{L}_G = \mathcal{L}_{\hat{a}} + \mathcal{L}_{\hat{t}},$$

where $M = N - K + 1$.

On the other hand, the dual discriminator D is training to distinguish between O and $\hat{O}$ by the following:

$$\mathcal{L}_a = \frac{1}{N}\sum_{i=1}^{N}(\log(1 - D_a(\hat{o}_i)) + \log(D_a(o_i))),$$

$$\mathcal{L}_t = \frac{1}{M}\sum_{i=1}^{M}(\log(1 - D_t(\{\hat{o}_i, ..., \hat{o}_{i+K-1}\})) \qquad (11)$$

$$+ \log(D_t(\{o_i, ..., o_{i+K-1}\}))),$$

$$\mathcal{L}_D = \mathcal{L}_a + \mathcal{L}_t.$$

Algorithm 1 multi-modal multi-level transformer (M³L)

1:   T: the multi-modal multi-level transformer
2:   U: the frame generator
3:   D: the dual discriminator, including D_a and D_t
4:   S: the source video, given instruction
5:   X: the given instruction
6:   O: the ground-truth target video
7:
8:   Initialize T, U, D
9:   **while** TRAINING **do**
10:     $\{v_1, ..., v_N\}$ = 3D ResNet(S)
11:     $e_X, \{e_{w_1}, ..., e_{w_N}\}$ = RoBERTa(X)
12:     **for** $i \leftarrow 1$ to N **do**   ▷ teacher-forcing training
13:       $d_i \leftarrow T(\{o_1, ..., o_{i-1}\}|v, \{e_X, e_w\})$ ▷ Eq. 7
14:       $\hat{o}_i \leftarrow U(d_i)$
15:       $\mathcal{L}_E \leftarrow$ visual difference loss with O ▷ Eq. 9
16:       $\mathcal{L}_G \leftarrow$ video quality loss from D ▷ Eq. 10
17:       Update T and U by minimizing $\mathcal{L}_G + \mathcal{L}_E$
18:       $\mathcal{L}_D \leftarrow$ discrimination loss for D ▷ Eq. 11
19:       Update D by maximizing $\mathcal{L}_D$
20:     **end for**
21: **end while**

Therefore, they are optimized through an alternating min-max game:

$$\min_{G}\max_{D} \mathcal{L}_G + \mathcal{L}_D. \qquad (12)$$

3.5. Learning of M³L

Algo. 1 presents the learning process of the proposed multi-modal multi-level transformer (M³L) for LBVE. Since LBVE is also a sequential generation process, we apply the widely used teacher-forcing training trick, where we feed in the ground-truth target frame o_{i-1} instead of the predicted $\hat{o}_{i-1}$ from the previous timestamp to make the training more robust. We adopt the multi-modal multi-level transformer T to model the source video and input instruction, and the frame generator U to generate the target video frame. During training, we minimize the video quality loss $\mathcal{L}_G$ with the visual difference $\mathcal{L}_E$ to optimize M³L. We also update the dual discriminator D, including the frame discriminator D_a and the temporal discriminator D_t, by maximizing $\mathcal{L}_D$. Therefore, the entire optimization object can be summarized as:

$$\min_{G,E}\max_{D} \mathcal{L}_G + \mathcal{L}_E + \mathcal{L}_D. \qquad (13)$$

4. Datasets

To the best of our knowledge, there is no dataset that supports video editing with the guided text. Therefore, we build three new datasets specially designed for LBVE, including two diagnostic datasets (E-MNIST and E-CLEVR) and one human gesture dataset (E-JESTER) for the language-based video editing (LBVE) task. An overview of our built

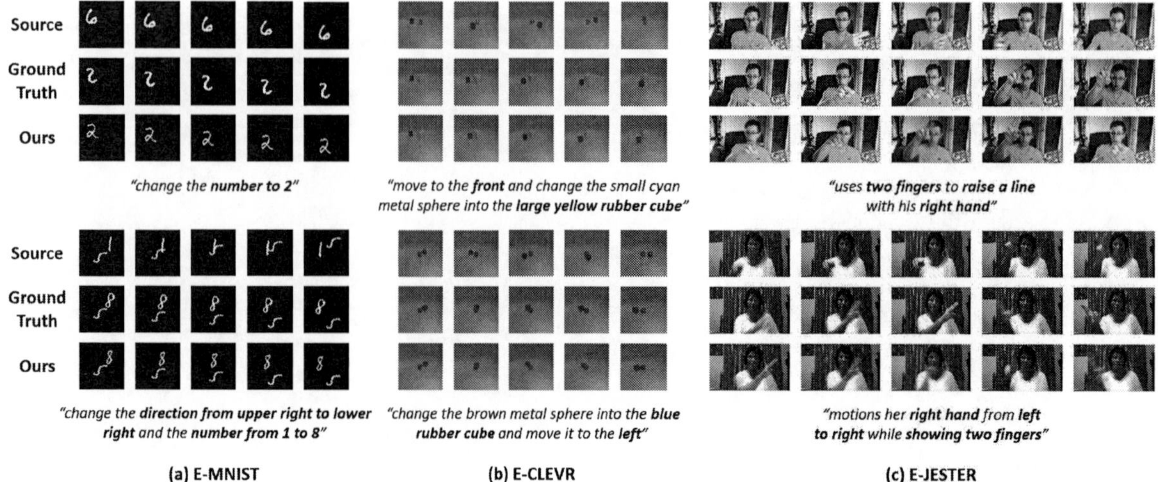

Figure 4. The sampled source videos, the ground-truth target videos, and the generated LBVE videos on all three datasets. More examples can be found on `https://lbvce2515.github.io/`.

datasets is shown in Table 1, and examples of these three datasets are illustrated in Fig. 4.

E-MNIST Extended from Moving MNIST [31, 53], the new E-MNIST dataset contains the instruction to describes the difference between two video clips. Hand-written numbers are moving along a specific direction and will reverse its direction if bumps into a boundary. The instructions include two kinds of editing actions: *content replacing* is to replace the specific number with the given one, and *semantic manipulation* changes the starting direction for different moving motion. We prepare two levels of E-MNIST, S-MNIST and D-MNIST. S-MNIST is an easier one and includes only a single number, so the model only needs to replace the number or change the moving direction at a time. There are two numbers in the advanced D-MNIST, where the model is required to perceive which number should be replaced and which starting direction should be changed simultaneously. For both S-MNIST and D-MNIST, there are 11,808 pairs of source-target video.

E-CLEVR Following CATER [16], we create each frame and combine them as the video in our E-CLEVR upon the original CLEVR dataset [26]. Each example consists of a pair of source-target videos with an instruction described the semantic altering. The editing action includes changing the property of the specific object and placing the moving object into a particular given final position. E-CLEVR contains plentiful object properties (e.g., color, shape, size, ...) and different relative positions of the final target. To highlight the importance of visual perception, not all aspects of the property will change; only the mentioned properties like the color and shape should be changed but keeps others the same. Besides, we will not always alter the moving object but sometimes the still one, where all clues are provided in the guided text. We generate 10,862 examples for the E-CLEVR dataset.

Dataset	#Train	#Test	#Frame	Avg. #Word	Resolution
S-MNIST	11,070	738	354,240	5.5	64x64
D-MNIST	11,070	738	354,240	16.0	64x64
E-CLEVR	9,233	1,629	21,7240	13.4	128x128
E-JESTER	14,022	885	59,508	9.9	100x176

Table 1. The statistics of our collected datsets.

E-JESTER Toward human action understanding, 20BN-JESTER [40] builds a large gesture recognition dataset. Each actor performs different kinds of gesture moving in front of the camera, which brings out 27 classes in total. This setting is appropriate to the video editing task where the source-target videos are under the same scenario (same person in the same environment) but with different semantics (different hand gestures). To support our LBVE task, we prepare pairs of clips from the same person as the source-target videos and collect the human-labeled instruction by Amazon Mechanical Turk (AMT)[1]. In this way, we can have the natural video whose scenario is preserved, but semantic is changing with natural guided text for our E-JESTER dataset, which can be a sufficient first step for LBVE. There are 14,907 pairs in E-JESTER.

5. Experiments

5.1. Experimental Setup

Evaluation Metrics
- **SSIM**: To compare the video similarity, we average the structural similarity index (SSIM) [65] value from all

---

[1] Amazon Mechanical Turk: `https://www.mturk.com/`

	S-MNIST			D-MNIST			E-CLEVR			E-JESTER			
	SSIM ↑	FAD ↓	VAD ↓	SSIM ↑	FAD ↓	VAD ↓	SSIM ↑	FAD ↓	VAD ↓	SSIM ↑	FAD ↓	VAD ↓	GA ↑
pix2pix [24]	86.0	1.31	2.06	63.7	2.13	3.05	80.1	2.05	2.84	74.6	1.62	2.00	8.6%
vid2vid [63]	90.0	0.96	1.30	82.0	1.51	2.30	94.0	1.45	2.21	82.0	1.50	1.62	82.0%
E3D-LSTM [64]	91.8	0.80	1.29	84.0	1.41	2.10	94.2	1.44	2.11	88.6	1.10	1.55	83.6%
M³L (Ours)	**93.2**	**0.80**	**1.28**	**87.9**	**1.24**	**1.90**	**96.8**	**1.32**	**1.96**	**91.7**	**1.04**	**1.44**	**89.3%**

Table 2. The overall testing results of the baselines and our M^3L under the E-MMIST, E-CLEVR, and E-JESTER datasets.

		E-JESTER			
Instruction	MLF	SSIM ↑	FAD ↓	VAD ↓	GA ↑
✗	✗	78.8	1.49	1.99	4.7%
✓	✗	89.6	1.16	1.50	85.4%
✓	✓	**91.7**	**1.04**	**1.44**	**89.3%**

Table 3. The ablation results when without the instruction or MLF.

	D-MNIST			E-CLEVR		
MLF	SSIM ↑	FAD ↓	VAD ↓	SSIM ↑	FAD ↓	VAD ↓
✗	72.89	1.91	2.64	86.61	1.70	2.32
✓	**77.84**	**1.75**	**2.35**	**90.07**	**1.51**	**2.29**

Table 4. The testing results of the zero-shot generalization.

frame pairs as the video SSIM.

- **FAD**: Similair to IS [51] and FID [21], frame activation distance (FAD) is computed by the mean L2 distance of the activations from the Inception V3 [54] feature. We treat the ground-truth target video as the reference. Because of being a distance metric, a lower FAD has a higher similarity between the two videos.
- **VAD**: Inspired by FVD [57], we apply the 3D CNN for more accurate video feature, and compute the video activation distance (VAD) following the same equation as FAD. Specifically, ResNeXt [68] is adopted for the diagnostic E-MNIST and E-CLEVR dataset. Besides, we utilize I3D [5] to extract the action video feature for E-JESTER. Similar to FAD, a lower VAD means that videos are more related to each other.
- **GA**: Apart from the visual-based evaluation, we report the gesture accuracy (GA) for E-JESTER. GA is calculated as the gesture classification accuracy of the edited video by MFFs[2] [29]. Although the generated video may not be totally the same as the ground truth, higher GA represents that the model is able to follow the guided text and generate the corresponding type of gesture.

Baselines Since our LBVE is a brand new task, there is no existing baselines. We consider following methods conditioning on an instruction, by concatenating the languistic feature with the hidden visual feature, to carry out LBVE as the compared baselines.

- **pix2pix** [24]: pix2pix is a supervised image-to-image translation approach. For the sake of video synthesis, we process the source video frame-by-frame to perform pix2pix.
- **vid2vid** [63]: vid2vid applies the temporal discriminator for better video-to-video synthesis, which considers several previous frames to model the translation.
- **E3D-LSTM** [64]: E3D-LSTM incorporates 3D CNN

---

[2]MFFs: https://github.com/okankop/MFF-pytorch

into LSTM for video prediction. We treat the source video as the given video and predict the remaining part as the target video.

5.2. Quantitative Results

Table 2 shows the overall testing results compared between the baselines and ours M^3L. pix2pix only adopts image-to-image translation, resulting in insufficient output video (e.g., 63.7 SSIM under D-MNIST and 2.84 VAD under E-CLEVR). Even if vid2vid and E3D-LSTM consider temporal consistency, the lack of explicit cross-modal fusion still makes them difficult to perform LBVE. While, our M^3L, which incorporates the multi-level fusion (MLF), can fuse between vision-and-language with different levels and surpass all baselines. In particular, M^3L achieves the best results across all metrics under all diagnostic datasets (e.g., 93.2 SSIM under S-MNIST, 1.24 FAD under D-MNIST, and 1.96 VAD under E-CLEVR).

Similar trends can be found on the natural E-JESTER dataset. pix2pix only has 8.6% GA, which shows that it cannot produce a video with the correct target gesture. Although vid2vid and E3D-LSTM may have similar visual measurement scores to our approach, M^3L achieves the highest 89.3% GA. The significant improvement of GA demonstrates that the proposed MLF benefits not only the visual quality but also the semantic of the predicted video and makes it more corresponding to the given instruction.

5.3. Ablation Study

Ablation Results Table 3 presents the testing results of the ablation setting under E-JESTER. If without the given instruction, the model lacks the specific editing target and results in poor 78.8 SSIM and 4.7% GA. The performance comprehensively improves when incorporating our proposed multi-level fusion (MLF) (e.g., VAD from 1.50 down to 1.44 and GA from 85.4% up to 89.3%). The multi-level modeling from MLF benefits not only the understanding be-

	w/ MLF	w/o MLF	Tie
Video Quality	**67.1%**	27.1%	5.8%
Video-Instruction Alignment	**53.3%**	35.1%	11.6%
Siml. to GT Video	**59.6%**	28.9%	11.6%

Table 5. Human evaluation on E-JESTER. Human judges evaluate video quality, video-instruction alignment, and similarity to GT video of the generated video w/ or w/o mutli-level fusion (MLF).

tween video and instruction, but also leads to accurate frame generation. The above ablation results show that the instruction is essential under the video editing task, and our MLF further helps to perform LBVE.

Zero-Shot Generalization To further investigate the generalizability of M^3L, we conduct a zero-shot experiment for both the D-MNIST and E-CLEVR datasets. In D-MNIST, there are 40 different object-semantic combinations[3]. We remove out 10 of them in the training set (e.g., number 1 with upper left or number 3 with lower down) and evaluate under the complete testing set. For E-CLEVR, we filter out 12 kinds (e.g., small gray metal sphere or large purple rubber cube) from the total 96 possibilities[4]. The results are shown in Table 4. Due to the lack of object properties or moving semantics, the model has a significant performance drop under the zero-shot settings. While, our proposed MLF helps the property and moving motion for both video perception and generation by multi-modal multi-level fusion. Therefore, MLF still improves the generalizability (e.g., VAD from 2.35 down to 2.29 under D-MNIST and SSIM from 86.6 up to 90.1 under E-CLEVR) even if training with the zero-shot examples.

Human Evaluation Apart from the quantitative results, we also investigate the quality of the generated video from the human aspect. Table 5 demonstrates the comparison between without and with MLF. We randomly sample 75 examples and ask three following questions: (1) Which video has better quality; (2) Which video corresponds more to the given instruction; (3) Which video is more similar to the ground-truth target video. Each example is assigned to 3 different MTurkers to avoid evaluation bias. Firstly, about 67% think that generated videos from MLF have better quality. Moreover, more than 50% of Mturkers denote that the target videos produced from MLF correspond more to the instruction and are also more similar to the ground truth. The results of the human evaluation indicate that our MLF not only helps improve the generating quality but also makes the target video more related to the guided text.

Multi-Level Fusion Fig. 5 illustrates the attention map from our multi-level fusion (MLF) under D-MNIST during frame decoding. The instruction tells to replacing the number 8 and change the moving direction of the number 5.

---

[3]**D-MNIST**: 10 different numbers and 4 different directions
[4]**E-CLEVR**: 3 shapes, 8 colors, 2 materials, and 2 shapes

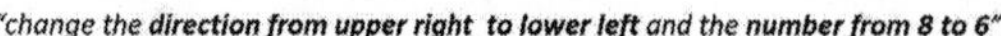

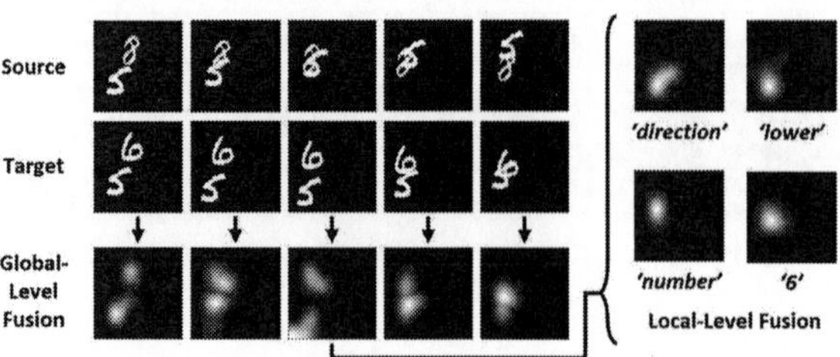

Figure 5. Visualization of the attention maps from the multi-level fusion (MLF) during decoding.

During decoding, the global-level fusion (GF) first gives the high-level video motion, and the attention maps reflect the moving directions for each output frame. Then, the local-level fusion (LF) helps extract perceived feature with respect to each word token. For instance of the 3rd frame, the word 'direction' and 'lower' are described for the number 5 of its moving direction. While, the tokens 'number' and '6' are responsible for replacing, thus they are attended on the position of the replaced number. With the cooperation of GF and LF, our MLF gives a concrete concept and brings out better target videos during the decoding.

5.4. Qualitative Results

Fig. 4 shows the keyframes of the generated examples of LBVE on all three datasets. For E-MNIST, we have to recognize which number should be replaced and which one will change the moving semantic. Note that the instruction only tells the replacing number, but without the style, thus our model replaces with another kind of number 2 under S-MNIST. Under the advanced D-MNIST dataset, our model can replace with the number 8 and move the number 5 along the lower right with multi-level fusion. The challenge of E-CLEVR is to transform object properties and move to the different target positions related to the fixed object. The visualization examples show that our model can understand the linguistic to change the specific object into the correct properties. Also, it has the spatial concept that can perceive the final related position and maintain the moving motion. The E-JESTER dataset, which contains nature video and human-labeled instruction, requires the link of the complex natural language with the human gesture action. The presented video indicates that our model can not only preserve a similar scenario (the background and the person) in the target video but also generate the visual motion of the corresponding gesture.

6. Conclusion

We introduce language-based video editing (LBVE), a novel task that allows the model to edit, guided by a natural text, a source video into a target video. We present multi-modal multi-level transformer (M^3L) to dynamically fuse video perception and language understanding at multiple levels. For the evaluation, we release three new datasets containing two diagnostic and one natural video with human-labeled text. Experimental results show that our M^3L is adequate for video editing, and LBVE can bring out a new field toward vision-and-language research.

References

[1] Ding Liu abd Zhaowen Wang, Yuchen Fan, Xianming Liu, Zhangyang Wang, Shiyu Chang, and Thomas Huang. Robust Video Super-Resolution with Learned Temporal Dynamics. In *ICCV*, 2017. 2

[2] Mohammad Babaeizadeh, Chelsea Finn, Dumitru Erhan, Roy H. Campbell, and Sergey Levine. Stochastic Variational Video Prediction. In *ICLR*, 2017. 2

[3] Yogesh Balaji, Martin Renqiang Min, Bing Bai, Rama Chellappa, and Hans Peter Graf. Conditional GAN with Discriminative Filter Generation for Text-to-Video Synthesis. In *IJCAI*, 2019. 1, 2

[4] Bert De Brabandere, Xu Jia, Tinne Tuytelaars, and Luc Van Gool. Dynamic Filter Networks. In *NeurIPS*, 2016. 2

[5] Joao Carreira and Andrew Zisserman. Quo Vadis, Action Recognition? A New Model and the Kinetics Dataset. In *CVPR*, 2017. 7

[6] Ya-Liang Chang, Zhe Liu Yu, , and Winston Hsu. VORNet: Spatio-temporally Consistent Video Inpainting for Object Removal. In *CVPR WS*, 2019. 2

[7] Devendra Singh Chaplot, Kanthashree Mysore Sathyendra, Rama Kumar Pasumarthi, Dheeraj Rajagopal, and Ruslan Salakhutdinov. Gated-Attention Architectures for Task-Oriented Language Grounding. In *AAAI*, 2018. 4

[8] Dongdong Chen, Jing Liao, Lu Yuan, Nenghai Yu, and Gang Hua. Coherent Online Video Style Transfer. In *ICCV*, 2017. 2

[9] Jianbo Chen, Yelong Shen, Jianfeng Gao, Jingjing Liu, and Xiaodong Liu. Language-Based Image Editing with Recurrent Attentive Models. In *CVPR*, 2018. 2

[10] Ming-Ming Cheng, Shuai Zheng, Wen-Yan Lin, Jonathan Warrell, Vibhav Vineet, Paul Sturgess, Nigel Crook, Niloy Mitra, and Philip Torr. ImageSpirit: Verbal Guided Image Parsing. In *ACM Transactions on Graphics*, 2013. 2

[11] Aidan Clark, Jeff Donahue, and Karen Simonyan. Adversarial Video Generation on Complex Datasets. In *arXiv:1907.06571*, 2019. 2, 5

[12] Yingying Deng, Fan Tang, Weiming Dong, Haibin Huang, Chongyang Ma, and Changsheng Xu. Arbitrary Video Style Transfer via Multi-Channel Correlation. In *AAAI*, 2021. 2

[13] Emily Denton and Rob Fergus. Stochastic Video Generation with a Learned Prior. In *ICML*, 2018. 2

[14] Alaaeldin El-Nouby, Shikhar Sharma, Hannes Schulz, Devon Hjelm, Layla El Asri, Samira Ebrahimi Kahou, Yoshua Bengio, and Graham W.Taylor. Tell, Draw, and Repeat: Generating and Modifying Images Based on Continual Linguistic Instruction. In *ICCV*, 2019. 2

[15] Tsu-Jui Fu, Xin Eric Wang, Scott Grafton, Miguel Eckstein, and William Yang Wang. SSCR: Iterative Language-Based Image Editing via Self-Supervised Counterfactual Reasoning. In *EMNLP*, 2020. 2

[16] Rohit Girdhar and Deva Ramanan. CATER: A diagnostic dataset for Compositional Actions and TEmporal Reasoning. In *ICLR*, 2020. 6

[17] Vincent Le Guen and Nicolas Thome. Disentangling Physical Dynamics from Unknown Factors for Unsupervised Video Prediction. In *CVPR*, 2020. 2

[18] Zekun Hao, Xun Huang, and Serge Belongie. Controllable Video Generation with Sparse Trajectories. In *CVPR*, 2018. 2

[19] Jiawei He, Andreas Lehrmann, Joseph Marino, Greg Mori, and Leonid Sigal. Probabilistic Video Generation using Holistic Attribute Control. In *ECCV*, 2018. 2

[20] Kaiming He, Xiangyu Zhang, Shaoqing Ren, and Jian Sun. Deep Residual Learning for Image Recognition. In *ICCV*, 2015. 4

[21] Martin Heusel, Hubert Ramsauer, Thomas Unterthiner, Bernhard Nessler, and Sepp Hochreiter. GANs Trained by a Two Time-Scale Update Rule Converge to a Local Nash Equilibrium. In *NeurIPS*, 2017. 7

[22] Jun-Ting Hsieh, Bingbin Liu, De-An Huang, Li Fei-Fei, and Juan Carlos Niebles. Learning to Decompose and Disentangle Representations for Video Prediction. In *NeurIPS*, 2018. 2

[23] Qiyang Hu, Adrian Waelchli, Tiziano Portenier, Matthias Zwicker, and Paolo Favaro. Video Synthesis from a Single Image and Motion Stroke. In *arXiv:1812.01874*, 2018. 2

[24] Phillip Isola, Jun-Yan Zhu, Tinghui Zhou, and Alexei A. Efros. Image-to-Image Translation with Conditional Adversarial Nets. In *CVPR*, 2017. 7

[25] Younghyun Jo, Seoung Wug Oh, Jaeyeon Kang, and Seon Joo Kim. Deep Video Super-Resolution Network Using Dynamic Upsampling Filters Without Explicit Motion Compensation. In *CVPR*, 2018. 2

[26] Justin Johnson, Bharath Hariharan, Laurens van der Maaten, Fei-Fei Li, Larry Zitnick, and Ross Girshick. CLEVR: A Diagnostic Dataset for Compositional Language and Elementary Visual Reasoning. In *CVPR*, 2017. 2, 6

[27] Nal Kalchbrenner, Aaron van den Oord, Karen Simonyan, Ivo Danihelka, Oriol Vinyals, Alex Graves, and Koray Kavukcuoglu. Video Pixel Networks. In *ICML*, 2017. 2

[28] Dahun Kim, Sanghyun Woo, Joon-Young Lee, and In So Kweon. Deep Video Inpainting. In *CVPR*, 2019. 2

[29] Okan Kopuklu and Neslihan Kose abd Gerhard Rigoll. Motion Fused Frames: Data Level Fusion Strategy for Hand Gesture Recognition. In *CVPR WS*, 2018. 7

[30] Gierad Laput, Mira Dontcheva, Gregg Wilensky, Walter Chang, Aseem Agarwala, Jason Linder, and Eytan Adar. PixelTone: A Multimodal Interface for Image Editing. In *CHI*, 2013. 2

[31] Yann LeCun, Corinna Cortes, and CJ Burges. MNIST Handwritten Digit Database. 2010. 2, 6

[32] Xuechen Li, Ting-Kam Leonard Wong, Ricky T. Q. Chen, and David Duvenaud. Scalable Gradients for Stochastic Differential Equations. In *AISTATS*, 2020. 2

[33] Yitong Li, Martin Renqiang Min, Dinghan Shen, David Carlson, and Lawrence Carin. Video Generation from Text. In *AAAI*, 2018. 1, 2

[34] Renjie Liao, Xin Tao, Ruiyu Li, Ziyang Ma, and Jiaya Jia. Video Super-Resolution via Deep Draft-Ensemble Learning. In *ICCV*, 2015. 2

[35] Chenxi Liu, Zhe Lin, Xiaohui Shen, Jimei Yang, Xin Lu, and Alan L Yuille. Recurrent Multimodal Interaction for Referring Image Segmentation. In *ICCV*, 2017. 4

[36] Ce Liu and Deqing Sun. A Bayesian Approach to Adaptive Video Super Resolution. In *CVPR*, 2011. 2

[37] Yinhan Liu, Myle Ott, Naman Goyal, Jingfei Du, Mandar Joshi, Danqi Chen, Omer Levy, Mike Lewis, Luke Zettlemoyer, and Veselin Stoyanov. RoBERTa: A Robustly Optimized BERT Pretraining Approach. In *arXiv:1907.11692*, 2019. 3

[38] Ziwei Liu, Raymond A. Yeh, Xiaoou Tang, and Aseem Agarwala Yiming Liu. Video Frame Synthesis using Deep Voxel Flow. In *ICCV*, 2017. 2

[39] Tanya Marwah, Gaurav Mittal, and Vineeth N. Balasubramanian. Attentive Semantic Video Generation using Captions. In *CVPR*, 2017. 1, 2

[40] Joanna Materzynska, Guillaume Berger, Ingo Bax, and Roland Memisevic. The Jester Dataset: A Large-Scale Video Dataset of Human Gestures. In *ICCV WS*, 2019. 6

[41] Michael Mathieu, Camille Couprie, and Yann LeCun. Deep Multi-Scale Video Prediction Beyond Mean Square Error. In *ICLR*, 2016. 2

[42] Takeru Miyato and Masanori Koyama. cGANs with Projection Discriminator. In *ICLR*, 2018. 5

[43] Anh Nguyen, Jeff Clune, Yoshua Bengio, Alexey Dosovitskiy, and Jason Yosinski. Plug & Play Generative Networks: Conditional Iterative Generation of Images in Latent Space. In *CVPR*, 2017. 2

[44] Yingwei Pan, Zhaofan Qiu, Ting Yao, Houqiang Li, and Tao Mei. To Create What You Tell: Generating Videos from Captions. In *ACMMM*, 2017. 1, 2

[45] Yunchen Pu, Martin Renqiang Min, Zhe Gan, and Lawrence Carin. Adaptive Feature Abstraction for Translating Video to Text. In *AAAI*, 2018. 2

[46] Fitsum A. Reda, Guilin Liu, Kevin J. Shih, Robert Kirby, Jon Barker, David Tarjan, Andrew Tao, and Bryan Catanzaro. SDC-Net: Video Prediction using Spatially-Displaced Convolution. In *ECCV*, 2018. 2

[47] Scott Reed, Zeynep Akata, Xinchen Yan, Lajanugen Logeswaran, Bernt Schiele, and Honglak Lee. Generative Adversarial Text to Image Synthesis. In *ICML*, 2016. 2

[48] Scott Reed, Aäron van den Oord, Nal Kalchbrenner, Sergio Gómez Colmenarejo, Ziyu Wang, Dan Belov, and Nando de Freitas. Parallel Multiscale Autoregressive Density Estimation. In *ICML*, 2017. 2

[49] Masaki Saito, Eiichi Matsumoto, and Shunta Saito. Temporal Generative Adversarial Nets with Singular Value Clipping. In *ICCV*, 2017. 2

[50] Masaki Saito and Shunta Saito. TGANv2: Efficient Training of Large Models for Video Generation with Multiple Subsampling Layers. In *arXiv:1811.09245*, 2018. 2

[51] Tim Salimans, Ian Goodfellow, Wojciech Zaremba, Vicki Cheung, Alec Radford, and Xi Chen. Improved Techniques for Training GANs. In *NeurIPS*, 2016. 7

[52] Seitaro Shinagawa, Koichiro Yoshino, Sakriani Sakti, Yu Suzuki, and Satoshi Nakamura. Interactive Image Manipulation with Natural Language Instruction Commands. In *NeurIPS WS*, 2017. 2

[53] Nitish Srivastava, Elman Mansimov, and Ruslan Salakhutdinov. Unsupervised Learning of Video Representations using LSTMs. In *ICML*, 2015. 2, 6

[54] Christian Szegedy, Vincent Vanhoucke, Sergey Ioffe, Jonathon Shlens, and Zbigniew Wojna. Rethinking the Inception Architecture for Computer Vision. In *CVPR*, 2016. 7

[55] Fuwen Tan, Song Feng, and Vicente Ordonez. Text2Scene: Generating Compositional Scenes from Textual Descriptions. In *CVPR*, 2019. 2

[56] Sergey Tulyakov, Ming-Yu Liu, Xiaodong Yang, and Jan Kautz. MoCoGAN: Decomposing Motion and Content for Video Generation. In *CVPR*, 2017. 2

[57] Thomas Unterthiner, Sjoerd van Steenkiste, Karol Kurach, Raphael Marinier, and Sylvain Gelly Marcin Michalski. Towards Accurate Generative Models of Video: A New Metric & Challenges. In *ICLR WS*, 2019. 7

[58] Ashish Vaswani, Noam Shazeer, Niki Parmar, Jakob Uszkoreit, Llion Jones, Aidan N. Gomez, Łukasz Kaiser, and Illia Polosukhin. Attention is All you Need. In *NeurIPS*, 2017. 4

[59] Ruben Villegas, Jimei Yang amd Seunghoon Hong, Xunyu Lin, and Honglak Lee. Decomposing Motion and Content for Natural Video Sequence Prediction. In *ICLR*, 2017. 2

[60] Carl Vondrick, Hamed Pirsiavash, and Antonio Torralba. Generating Videos with Scene Dynamics. In *NeurIPS*, 2016. 2

[61] Jacob Walker, Ali Razavi, and Aäron van den Oord. Predicting Video with VQVAE. In *arXiv:2103.01950*, 2021. 2

[62] Ting-Chun Wang, Ming-Yu Liu, Andrew Tao, Guilin Liu, Jan Kautz, and Bryan Catanzaro. Few-shot Video-to-Video Synthesis. In *NeurIPS*, 2019. 2

[63] Ting-Chun Wang, Ming-Yu Liu, Jun-Yan Zhu, Guilin Liu, Andrew Tao, Jan Kautz, and Bryan Catanzaro. Video-to-Video Synthesis. In *NeurIPS*, 2018. 2, 7

[64] Yunbo Wang, Lu Jiang, Ming-Hsuan Yang, Li-Jia Li, Mingsheng Long, and Li Fei-Fei. Eidetic 3D LSTM: A Model for Video Prediction and Beyond. In *ICLR*, 2019. 7

[65] Zhou Wang, Alan Bovik, Hamid Rahim Sheikh, and Eero P. Simoncelli. Image Quality Assessment: From Error Visibility to Structural Similarity. In *Transactions on Image Processing*, 2004. 6

[66] Dirk Weissenborn, Oscar Täckström, and Jakob Uszkoreit. Scaling Autoregressive Video Models. In *ICLR*, 2020. 2

[67] Xide Xia, Tianfan Xue, Wei-Sheng Lai, Zheng Sun, Abby Chang, Brian Kulis, and Jiawen Chen. Real-Time Localized Photorealistic Video Style Transfer. In *WACV*, 2021. 2

[68] Saining Xie, Ross Girshick, Piotr Dollár, Zhuowen Tu, and Kaiming He. Aggregated Residual Transformations for Deep Neural Networks. In *CVPR*, 2017. 7

[69] Kelvin Xu, Jimmy Ba, Ryan Kiros, Kyunghyun Cho, Aaron Courville, Ruslan Salakhutdinov, Richard Zemel, and Yoshua Bengio. Show, Attend and Tell: Neural Image Caption Generation with Visual Attention. In *ICML*, 2015. 4

[70] Rui Xu, Xiaoxiao Li, Bolei Zhou, and Chen Change Loy. Deep Flow-Guided Video Inpainting. In *CVPR*, 2019. 2

[71] Tao Xu, Pengchuan Zhang, Qiuyuan Huang, Han Zhang, Zhe Gan, Xiaolei Huang, and Xiaodong Hes. AttnGAN: Fine-Grained Text to Image Generation with Attentional Generative Adversarial Networks. In *CVPR*, 2018. 2

[72] Linwei Ye, Mrigank Rochan, Zhi Liu, and Yang Wang. Cross-Modal Self-Attention Network for Referring Image Segmentation. In *CVPR*, 2019. 4

[73] Han Zhang, Ian Goodfellow, Dimitris Metaxas, and Augustus Odena. Self-Attention Generative Adversarial Networks. In *PMLR*, 2019. 4

[74] Han Zhang, Tao Xu, Hongsheng Li, Shaoting Zhang, Xiaogang Wang, Xiaolei Huang, and Dimitris Metaxas. StackGAN: Text to Photo-realistic Image Synthesis with Stacked Generative Adversarial Networkss. In *ICCV*, 2017. 2

Pathdreamer: A World Model for Indoor Navigation

Jing Yu Koh[1] Honglak Lee[2] Yinfei Yang[1] Jason Baldridge[1] Peter Anderson[1]

[1]Google Research [2]University of Michigan

Abstract

People navigating in unfamiliar buildings take advantage of myriad visual, spatial and semantic cues to efficiently achieve their navigation goals. Towards equipping computational agents with similar capabilities, we introduce Pathdreamer, a visual world model for agents navigating in novel indoor environments. Given one or more previous visual observations, Pathdreamer generates plausible high-resolution 360° visual observations (RGB, semantic segmentation and depth) for viewpoints that have not been visited, in buildings not seen during training. In regions of high uncertainty (e.g. predicting around corners, imagining the contents of an unseen room), Pathdreamer can predict diverse scenes, allowing an agent to sample multiple realistic outcomes for a given trajectory. We demonstrate that Pathdreamer encodes useful and accessible visual, spatial and semantic knowledge about human environments by using it in the downstream task of Vision-and-Language Navigation (VLN). Specifically, we show that planning ahead with Pathdreamer brings about half the benefit of looking ahead at actual observations from unobserved parts of the environment. We hope that Pathdreamer will help unlock model-based approaches to challenging embodied navigation tasks such as navigating to specified objects and VLN.

1. Introduction

World models [23], or models of environments [72], are an appealing way to represent an agent's knowledge about its surroundings. An agent with a world model can predict its future by 'imagining' the consequences of a series of proposed actions. This capability can be used for sampling-based planning [16, 57], learning policies directly from the model (i.e., learning in a dream) [17, 23, 64, 25], and for counterfactual reasoning [6]. Model-based approaches such as these also typically improve the sample efficiency of deep reinforcement learning [72, 62]. However, world models that generate high-dimensional visual observations (i.e., images) have typically been restricted to relatively simple environments, such as Atari games [62] and tabletops [16].

Our goal is to develop a generic visual world model for agents navigating in indoor environments. Specifically,

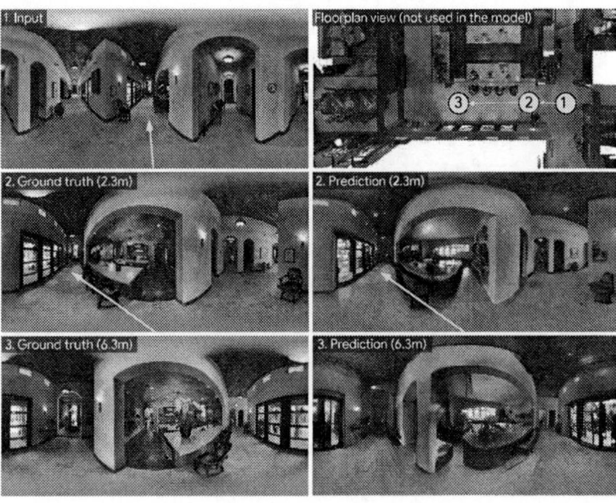

Figure 1: Generating photorealistic 360° visual observations from an imagined 6.3m trajectory in a previously unseen building. Observations also include depth and segmentations (not shown here).

given one or more previous observations and a proposed navigation action sequence, we aim to generate plausible high-resolution visual observations for viewpoints that have not been visited, and do so in buildings not seen during training. Beyond applications in video editing and content creation, solving this problem would unlock model-based methods for many embodied AI tasks, including navigating to objects [5], instruction-guided navigation [3, 66, 40] and dialog-guided navigation [74, 26]. For example, an agent asked to find a certain type of object in a novel building, e.g. *'find a chair'*, could perform mental simulations using the world model to identify navigation trajectories that are most likely to include chair observations – without moving.

Building such a model is challenging. It requires synthesizing completions of partially visible objects, using as few as one previous observation. This is akin to novel view synthesis from a single image [19, 80], but with potentially unbounded viewpoint changes. There is also the related but considerably more extreme challenge of predicting around corners. For example, as shown in Fig. 1, any future navigation trajectory passing the entrance of an unseen room requires the model to plausibly imagine the entire contents

Proceedings of the Second Workshop on Advances in Language and Vision Research, pages 57–67

of that room (we dub this the *room reveal* problem). This requires generalizing from the visual, spatial and semantic structure of previously explored environments—which in our case are photo-realistic 3D captures of real indoor spaces in the Matterport3D dataset [7]. A third problem is temporal consistency: predictions of unseen building regions should ideally be stochastic (capturing the full distribution of possible outcomes), but revisited regions should be rendered in a consistent manner to previous observations.

Towards this goal, we introduce Pathdreamer. Given one or more visual observations (consisting of RGB, depth and semantic segmentation for panoramas) from an indoor scene, Pathdreamer synthesizes high-resolution visual observations (RGB, depth and semantic segmentations) along a specified trajectory through future viewpoints, using a hierarchical two-stage approach. Pathdreamer's first stage, Structure Generator, generates depth and semantic segmentations. Inspired by work in video prediction [11], these outputs are conditioned on a latent noise tensor capturing the stochastic information about the next observation (such as the layout of an unseen room) that cannot be predicted deterministically. The second stage's Image Generator renders the depth and semantic segmentations as realistic RGB images using modified Multi-SPADE blocks [63, 51]. To maintain long-term consistency in the generated observations, both stages use back-projected 3D point cloud representations which are re-projected into image space for context [51].

As illustrated in Figure 1, Pathdreamer can generate plausible views of previously unseen indoor scenes under large viewpoint changes, while also addressing the *room reveal* problem – in this case correctly hypothesizing that the unseen room revealed at position 2 will most likely resemble a kitchen. Empirically, using the Matterport3D dataset [7] and 360° observations, we evaluate both stages of our model against prior work and reasonable baselines and ablations. We find that the hierarchical structure of the model is essential for predicting over large viewpoint changes, that maintaining both RGB and semantic context is required, and that prediction quality degrades gradually when we evaluate with trajectory rollouts of up to 13m (with viewpoints 2.25m apart on average).

Encouraged by these results, we further evaluate whether RGB predictions from Pathdreamer can improve performance on a downstream visual navigation task. We focus on Vision-and-Language Navigation (VLN) using the R2R dataset [3]. VLN requires agents to interpret and execute natural language navigation instructions in a photorealistic 3D environment. A robust finding from previous VLN research is that task success is dramatically increased by allowing an agent to look ahead at unobserved parts of the environment while following an instruction [50]. We find that replacing look-ahead observations with Pathdreamer pre-

dictions maintains around half of this improvement, a finding we expect to have significant implications for research in this area. In summary, our main contributions include:

- Proposing the study of visual world models for generic indoor environments and defining evaluation protocols and baselines for future work.
- Pathdreamer, a stochastic hierarchical visual world model combining multiple, independent threads of previous work on video prediction [11], semantic image synthesis [63] and video-to-video synthesis [51].
- Extensive experiments characterizing the performance of Pathdreamer and demonstrating improved results on the downstream VLN task [3].

2. Related Work

Video Prediction Our work is closely related to the task of video prediction, which aims to predict the future frames of a video sequence. While some video prediction methods predict RGB video frames directly [76, 1, 41, 44], many others use hierarchical models to first predict an intermediate representation (such as semantic segmentation) [47, 35, 77, 82, 42], which improves the fidelity of long-term predictions [42]. Several approaches have also incorporated 3D point cloud representations, using projective camera geometry to explicitly infer aspects of the next frame [75, 51, 43]. Inspired by this work, we adopt and combine both the hierarchical two-stage approach and 3D point cloud representations. Further, since our interest is in action-conditional world models, we provide a trajectory of future viewpoints to the model rather than assuming a constant frame rate and modeling camera motion implicitly, which is more typical in video generation [44, 42].

Action-Conditional Video Prediction Conditional video prediction to improve agent reasoning and planning has been explored in several tasks. This includes video prediction for Atari games conditioned on control inputs [60, 10, 62, 25] and 3D game environments like Doom [23]. In robotics, action-conditional video prediction has been investigated for object pushing in tabletop settings to improve generalization to novel objects [15, 16, 14]. This work has been restricted to simple environments and low-resolution images, such as 64×64 images of objects in a wooden box. To the best of our knowledge, we are the first to investigate action-conditional video prediction in building-scale environments with high-resolution (1024×512) images.

World Models and Navigation Priors World models [23] are an appealing way to summarize and distill knowledge about complex, high-dimensional environments. However, world models can differ in their outputs. While Pathdreamer predicts visual observations, there is also a vast literature on world models that predict compact latent representations of future states [38, 24, 25] or other task-specific measurements [13] or rewards [61]. This includes recent work attempting to learn statistical regularities and other priors for indoor navigation—for example, by mining spatial co-occurrences from real estate video tours [8], learning to predict top-down belief maps over room characteristics [58], or learning to reconstruct house floor plans using audio and visual cues from a short video sequence [65]. In contrast to these approaches, we focus on explicitly predicting visual observations (i.e., pixels) which are generic, human-interpretable, and apply to a wide variety of downstream tasks and applications. Further, recent work identifies a close correlation between image prediction accuracy and downstream task performance in model-based RL [4].

Embodied Navigation Agents High-quality 3D environment datasets such as Matterport3D [7], StreetLearn [56, 53], Gibson [81] and Replica [71] have triggered intense interest in developing embodied agents that act in realistic human environments [2]. Tasks of interest include Object-Nav [5] (navigating to an instance of a particular kind of object), and Vision-and-Language Navigation (VLN) [3], in which agents must navigate according to natural language instructions. Variations of VLN include indoor navigation [3, 33, 66, 40], street-level navigation [9, 53], vision-and-dialog navigation [59, 74, 26], VLN in continuous environments [39], and more. Notwithstanding considerable exploration of pretraining strategies [46, 27, 50, 87], data augmentation approaches [20, 21, 73], agent architectures and loss functions [86, 48, 49], existing work in this space considers only model-free approaches. Our aim is to unlock model-based approaches to these tasks, using a visual world model to encode prior commonsense knowledge about human environments and thereby relieve the burden on the agent to learn these regularities. Underscoring the potential of this direction, we note that using the ground-truth environment for planning with beam search typically improves VLN success rates on the R2R dataset by 17-19% [20, 73].

Novel View Synthesis Finally, we position our work in the context of novel view synthesis [19, 37, 29, 18, 70, 85, 54]. Many methods have been proposed to represent 3D scenes, including point cloud representations [80], layered depth images [12], and mesh representations [68]. More recently, neural radiance fields (NeRF) [55, 52, 83] achieved impressive results by capturing volume density and color implicitly with a neural network. NeRF models can synthesize very high quality 3D scenes, but a significant drawback for our purposes is that they require a large number of input views to render a single scene (e.g., 20–62 images per scene in [55]). More importantly, these models are typically trained to represent a single scene, and currently do not generalize well to unseen environments. In contrast, our problem demands generalization to unseen environments, using as little as one previous observation.

3. Pathdreamer

Pathdreamer is a world model that generates high-resolution visual observations from a trajectory of future viewpoints in buildings it has never observed. The input to Pathdreamer is a sequence of previous observations consisting of RGB images $I_{1:t-1}$, semantic segmentation images $s_{1:t-1}$, and depth images $d_{1:t-1}$ (where the depth and segmentations could be ground-truth or estimates from a model). We assume that a corresponding sequence of camera poses $T_{1:t-1}$ is available from an odometry system, and that the camera intrinsics are known or estimated. Our goal is to generate realistic RGB, semantic segmentation and depth images for a trajectory of future poses $T_t, T_{t+1}, \ldots, T_T$, which may be provided up front or iteratively by some agent interacting with the returned observations. Note that we generate depth and segmentation because these modalities are useful in many downstream tasks. We assume that the future trajectory may traverse unseen areas of environment, requiring the model to not only in-fill minor object dis-occlusions, but also to imagine entire room reveals (Figure 1).

Figure 2 shows our proposed hierarchical two-stage model for addressing this challenge. It uses a latent noise tensor z_t to capture the stochastic information about the next observation (e.g. the layout of an unseen room) that cannot be predicted deterministically. Given a sampled noise tensor z_t, the first stage (Structure Generator) generates a new depth image $\hat{d}_t$ and segmentation image $\hat{s}_t$ to provide a plausible high-level semantic representation of the scene, using as context the previous semantic and depth images $s_{1:t-1}$, $d_{1:t-1}$. In the second stage (Image Generator), the predicted semantic and depth images $\hat{s}_t$, $\hat{d}_t$ are rendered into a realistic RGB image $\hat{I}_t$ using previous RGB images $I_{1:t-1}$ as context. In each stage, context is provided by accumulating previous observations as a 3D point cloud which is re-projected into 2D using T_t.

3.1. Structure Generator: Segmentation & Depth

Pathdreamer's first stage is the Structure Generator, a stochastic encoder-decoder network for generating diverse, plausible segmentation and depth images. Like [51], to provide the previous observation context, we first back-project the previous segmentations $s_{1:t-1}$ into a unified 3D semantic point cloud using the depth images $d_{1:t-1}$ and camera poses $T_{1:t-1}$. We then re-project this point cloud back into pixel space using T_t to create sparse segmentation and depth guidance images s_t', d_t' which reflect the current pose.

The input to the encoder is a one-hot encoding of the semantic guidance image $s_t' \in \mathbb{R}^{W \times H \times C}$, concatenated with the depth guidance image $d_t' \in \mathbb{R}^{W \times H \times 1}$. The architecture of the encoder-decoder model is based on RedNet [34] – a ResNet-50 [28] architecture designed for indoor RGB-D semantic segmentation. RedNet uses transposed convolu-

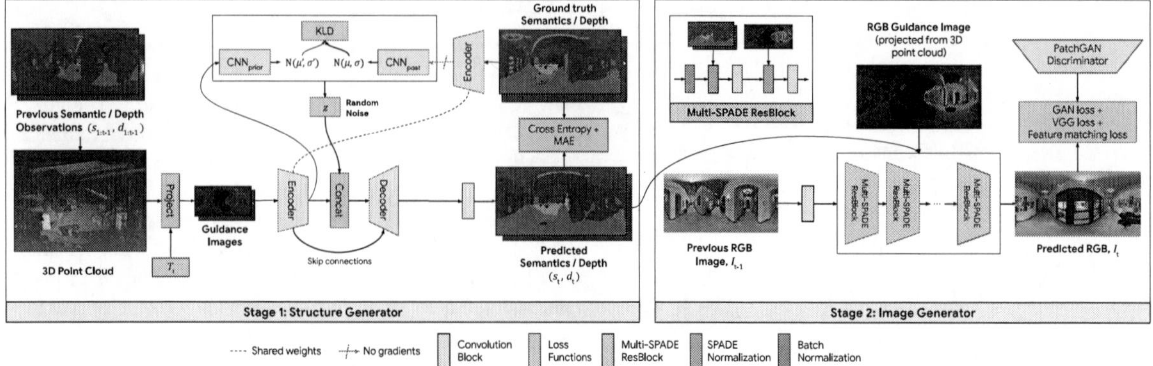

Figure 2: Pathdreamer model architecture at step t. Given a history of visual observations (RGB, depth and semantics) and a trajectory of future viewpoints, the Structure Generator conditions on a sampled noise tensor before generating semantic and depth outputs to provide a high-level structural representation of the scene. Realistic RGB images are synthesized by the Image Generator in the second stage.

tions for upsampling in the decoder and skip connections between the encoder and decoder to preserve spatial information. Since the input contains a segmentation image, and segmentation classes differ across datasets, the encoder-decoder is not pretrained. We introduce the latent spatial noise tensor $z_t \in \mathbb{R}^{H' \times W' \times 32}$ into the model by concatenating it with the feature map between the encoder and the decoder. The final output of the encoder-decoder model is a segmentation image $\hat{s}_t$ and a depth image $\hat{d}_t$, with segmentation predictions generated by a C-way softmax and depth outputs normalized in the range $(0, 1)$ and generated via a sigmoid function. At each step during inference, the segmentation prediction $\hat{s}_t$ is back-projected and added to the point cloud to assist prediction in future timesteps.

To generate the noise tensor z_t, we take inspiration from SVG [11] and learn a conditional prior noise distribution $p_\psi(z_t|s'_t, d'_t)$. Intuitively, there are many possible scenes that may be generated for an unseen building region. We would like z_t to carry the stochastic information about the next observation that the deterministic encoder cannot capture, and we would like for the decoder to make good use of that information. During training, we encourage the first outcome by using a KL-divergence loss to force the prior distribution $p_\psi(z_t|s'_t, d'_t)$ to be close to the posterior distribution $\phi(z_t|s_t, d_t)$ which is conditioned on the ground-truth segmentation and depth images. We encourage the second outcome by providing the decoder with sampled z_t values from the posterior distribution q_ϕ (conditioned on the ground-truth outputs) during training. During inference, the latent noise z_t is sampled from the prior distribution p_ψ and the posterior distribution q_ϕ is not used. Both distributions are modeled using 3-layer CNNs that take their input from the encoder and output two channels representing μ and σ to parameterize a multivariate Gaussian distribution $\mathcal{N}(\mu, \sigma)$. As shown in Figure 3, the noise is useful in encoding di-

verse, plausible representations of unseen regions.

Overall, the Structure Generator is trained to minimize a joint loss consisting of a cross-entropy loss L_{ce} for semantic predictions, a mean absolute error term for depth predictions, and the KL-divergence term for the noise tensor:

$$\mathcal{L}_{\text{Structure}} = \lambda_{ce} L_{ce}(s_t, \hat{s}_t)$$
$$+ \lambda_d \left\| d_t - \hat{d}_t \right\|_1$$
$$+ \lambda_{\text{KL}} D_{\text{KL}}\big(q_\phi(z_t|s_t, d_t), p_\psi(z_t|s'_t, d'_t)\big) \quad (1)$$

where λ_{ce}, λ_d, and λ_{KL} are weights determined by a grid search. We set these to 1, 100, and 0.5 respectively.

3.2. Image Generator: RGB

The Image Generator is an image-to-image translation GAN [22, 78] that converts the semantic and depth predictions $\hat{s}_t$, $\hat{d}_t$ from the first stage into a realistic RGB image $\hat{I}_t$. Our model architecture is based on SPADE blocks [63] that use spatially-adaptive normalization layers to insert context into multiple layers of the network. As with our Structure Generator, we maintain an accumulating 3D point cloud containing all previous image observations. This provides a sparse RGB guidance image I'_t when re-projected. Similar to Multi-SPADE [51], we insert two SPADE normalization layers into each residual block: one conditioned on the concatenated semantic and depth inputs $[\hat{s}_t, \hat{d}_t]$, and one conditioned on the RGB guidance image I'_t. The sparsity of the RGB guidance image is handled by applying partial convolutions [45]. In total Image Generator consists of 7 Multi-SPADE blocks, preceded by a single convolution block.

Following SPADE [63], the model is trained with the GAN hinge loss, feature matching loss [78], and perceptual loss [36] from a pretrained VGG-19 [69] model. During training, the generator is provided with the ground-truth segmentation image s_t and ground-truth depth image d_t.

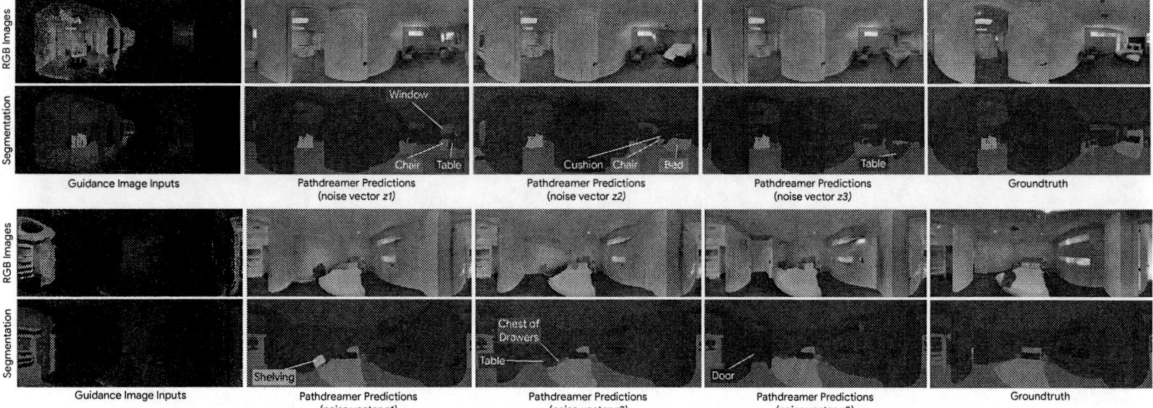

Figure 3: When predicting around corners, the Structure Generator can sample diverse and semantically plausible scene layouts which are closely reflected in the RGB output of the Image Generator, shown here for two guidance image inputs (left columns; unseen areas are indicated by solid black regions). Each example shows three alternative *room reveals* and the groundtruth. In the bottom example, the model considers various completions for a bedroom but fails to anticipate the groundtruth's matching lamp on the opposite side of the bed.

Our discriminator architecture is based on PatchGAN [32], and takes as input the concatenation of the ground-truth image I_t or generated image $\hat{I}_t$, the ground-truth depth image d_t and the ground-truth semantic image s_t. The losses for the generator G and the discriminator D are:

$$\mathcal{L}_G = -\lambda_{\text{GAN}}\mathbb{E}_{x_t}\left[D(G(x_t))\right]$$
$$+ \lambda_{\text{VGG}}\sum_{i=1}^{n}\frac{1}{n}\left\|\phi^{(i)}(I_t) - \phi^{(i)}(G(x_t))\right\|_1$$
$$+ \lambda_{\text{FM}}\sum_{i}^{n}\frac{1}{n}\left\|D^{(i)}(I_t) - D^{(i)}(G(x_t))\right\|_1 \quad (2)$$
$$\mathcal{L}_D = -\mathbb{E}_{x_t}\left[\min(0, -1 + D(I_t))\right]$$
$$- \mathbb{E}_{x_t}\left[\min(0, -1 - D(G(x_t)))\right] \quad (3)$$

where $x_t = (s_t, d_t, I'_t)$ denotes the complete set of inputs to the generator, $\phi^{(i)}$ denotes the intermediate output of the ith layer of the pretrained VGG-19 network, $D^{(i)}$ denotes the output of the discriminator's i-th layer, and the conditioning inputs s_t, d_t to the discriminator have been dropped to save space. We follow [63] for the choice of weights λ. Like the Structure Generator, the Image Generator is not pretrained.

3.3. Training and Inference

Dataset For training and evaluation we use Matterport3D [7], a dataset of 10.8k RGB-D images from 90 building-scale indoor environments. For each environment, Matterport3D also includes a textured 3D mesh which is annotated with 40 semantic classes of objects and building components. To align with downstream VLN tasks, in all experiments the RGB, depth and semantic images are 360° panoramas in equirectangular format.

Trajectories To train Pathdreamer, we sampled 400k trajectories from the Matterport3D training environments. To define feasible trajectories, we used the navigation graphs from the Room-to-Room (R2R) dataset [3], in which nodes correspond to panoramic image locations, and edges define navigable state transitions. For each trajectory 5–8 panoramas were sampled, choosing the starting node and the edge transitions uniformly at random. On average the viewpoints in these trajectories are 2m apart. Training with relatively large viewpoint changes is desirable, since the model learns to synthesize observations with large viewpoint changes in a single step (without the need to incur the computational cost of generating intervening frames). However, this does not preclude Pathdreamer from generating smooth video outputs at high frame rates[1].

Training The first and second stages of the model are trained separately. For the Image Generator, we use the Matterport3D RGB panoramas as training targets at 1024×512 resolution. We use the Habitat simulator [67] to render ground-truth depth and semantic training inputs and stitch these into equirectangular panoramas. We perform data augmentation by randomly cropping and horizontally rolling the RGB panoramas, which we found essential due to the limited number of panoramas available.

To train the Structure Generator, we again used Habitat to render depth and semantic images. Since this stage does not require aligned RGB images for training, in this case we performed data augmentation by perturbing the viewpoint coordinates with a random Gaussian noise vector drawn from $\mathcal{N}(0, 0.2\text{m})$ independently along each 3D

---

[1]See https://youtu.be/HNAmsdk71J4 for our video generation results.

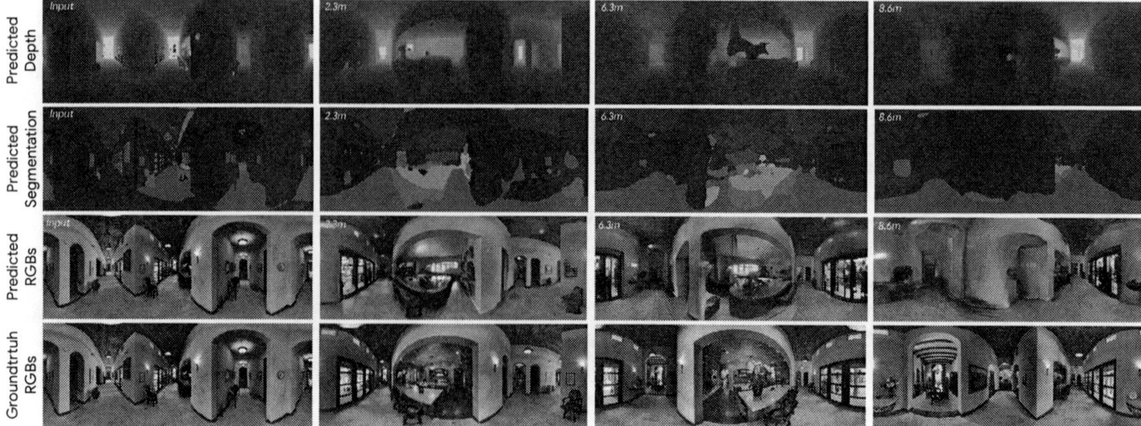

Figure 4: Example full prediction sequence beginning with one observation (depth, semantics, RGB) as context and generating observations for 3 new viewpoints traversing a corridor. At 2.3m the model completes a room reveal, imagining a kitchen-like space. After 8.6m the model's predictions degrade. More examples are provided in the supplementary.

axis. The Structure Generator was trained with equirectangular panoramas at 512×256 resolution.

Inference   To avoid heading discontinuities during inference, we use circular padding on the image x-axis for both the Structure Generator and the Image Generator. The 512×256 resolution semantic and depth outputs of the Structure Generator are upsampled to 1024×512 using nearest neighbor interpolation before they are passed to the Image Generator. In quantitative experiments, we set the Structure Generator noise tensor z_t to the mean of the prior.

4. Experiments

For evaluation we use the paths from the Val-Seen and Val-Unseen splits of the R2R dataset [3]. Val-Seen contains 340 trajectories from environments in the Matterport3D training split. Val-Unseen contains 783 trajectories in Matterport3D environments not seen in training. Since R2R trajectories contain 5-7 panoramas and at least 1 previous observation is given as context, we report evaluations over 1–6 steps, representing predictions over trajectory rollouts of around 2–13m (panoramas are 2.25m apart on average). See Figure 4 for an example rollout over 8.6m. We characterize the performance of Pathdreamer in comparison to baselines, ablations and in the context of the downstream task of Vision-and-Language Navigation (VLN).

4.1. Pathdreamer Results

Semantic Generation   A key feature of our approach is the ability to generate semantic segmentation and depth outputs, in addition to RGB. We evaluate the generated semantic segmentation images using mean Intersection-Over-Union (mIOU) and report results for:

- **Nearest Neighbor**: A baseline without any learned components, using nearest-neighbor interpolation to fill holes in the projected semantic guidance image s'_t.

- **Ours (Teacher Forcing)**: Structure Generator trained using the ground truth semantic and depth images as the previous observation at every time step.
- **Ours (Recurrent)**: Structure Generator trained while feeding back its own semantic and depth predictions as previous observations for the next step prediction. This reduces train-test mismatch and may allow the model to compensate for errors when doing longer roll-outs.

We also tried training the hierarchical convolutional LSTM from [42], but found that it frequently collapsed to a single class prediction. We attribute this to the large viewpoint changes and heavy occlusion in the training sequences; we believe this can be more effectively modeled with point cloud geometry than with a geometry-unaware LSTM.

As illustrated in Table 1, Pathdreamer performs far better than the Nearest Neighbor baseline regardless of the number of steps in the rollout or the number of previous observations used as context. As expected, performance in seen environments is higher than unseen. Perhaps surprisingly, in Figure 5a we show that Recurrent training improves results during longer rollouts in the training environments (Val-Seen), but this does not improve results on Val-Unseen, perhaps indicating that the error compensation learned by the Image Generator does not easily generalize.

In addition to accurate predictions, we also want generated results to be *diverse*. Figure 3 shows that our model can generate diverse semantic scenes by interpolating the noise tensor z_t, and that the RGB outputs closely reflect the generated semantic image. This allows us to generate multiple plausible alternatives for the same navigation trajectory.

RGB Generation   To evaluate the quality of RGB panoramas generated by the Image Generator, we compute the Fréchet Inception Distance (FID) [30] between generated and real images for each step in the paths. We report re-

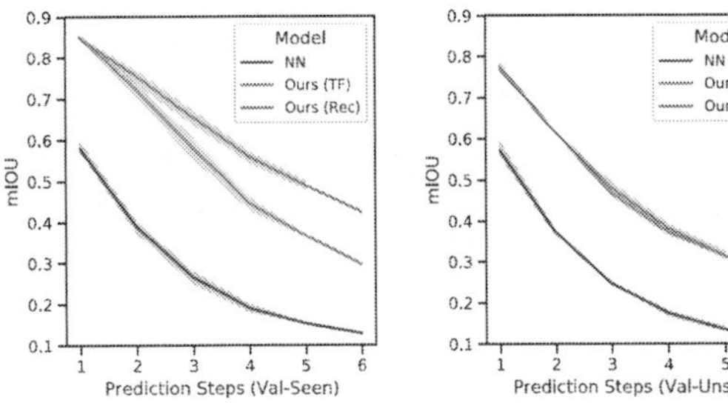

(a) Semantic segmentation mean-IOU (↑). **[TF]**: Teacher Forcing. **[Rec]**: Recurrent.

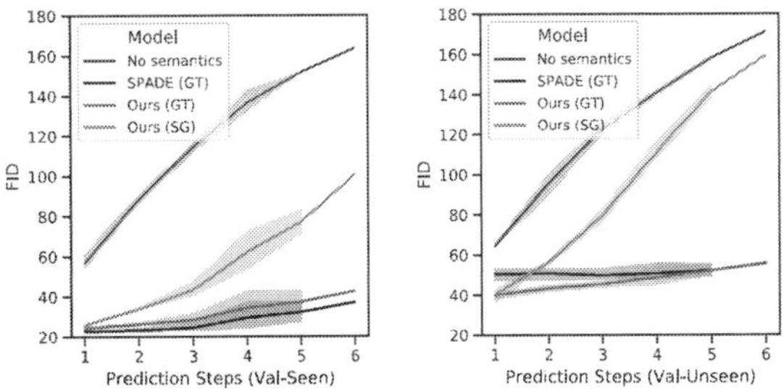

(b) RGB generation FID (↓). **[GT]**: Ground truth semantic inputs. **[SG]**: Structure Generator predictions.

Figure 5: Pathdreamer semantic segmentation mean-IOU (above) and RGB generation FID (below). Results are shown for Val-Seen (left) and Val-Unseen (right). Confidence intervals indicate the range of outcomes with 1, 2 or 3 previous observations as context.

		Val-Seen		Val-Unseen	
Model	Context	1 Step	1–6 Steps	1 Step	1–6 Steps
Nearest Neighbor	1	59.5	32.0	59.1	30.6
Ours (Teacher Forcing)	1	**84.9**	59.2	**78.3**	50.8
Ours (Recurrent)	1	84.7	**65.9**	77.5	**50.9**
Nearest Neighbor	2	57.4	35.2	56.5	33.8
Ours (Teacher Forcing)	2	**85.4**	64.6	**77.4**	55.5
Ours (Recurrent)	2	85.1	**70.2**	76.6	**55.7**
Nearest Neighbor	3	57.4	38.7	56.1	37.7
Ours (Teacher Forcing)	3	**85.1**	68.5	**77.3**	60.4
Ours (Recurrent)	3	84.6	**72.7**	76.8	**60.8**

Table 1: Mean-IOU (↑) for generated semantic segmentations with varying context and prediction steps.

		Inputs			Val-Seen		Val-Unseen	
Model	Context	Obs	Sem	RGB	1 Step	1–6 Steps	1 Step	1–6 Steps
No Semantics	1		-	✓	61.2	112.1	64.0	117.8
SPADE	1		GT	✓	**23.3**	**24.9**	47.3	50.3
Ours	1		GT	✓ ✓	25.1	28.6	37.9	**45.2**
Ours	1		SG	✓ ✓	26.2	48.3	**36.6**	85.5
No Semantics	2		-	✓	54.2	98.9	65.6	107.4
SPADE	2		GT	✓	**22.8**	**25.3**	52.3	51.2
Ours	2		GT	✓ ✓	24.4	28.6	**41.3**	**44.9**
Ours	2		SG	✓ ✓	25.7	42.6	41.8	74.7
No Semantics	3		-	✓	54.9	89.8	64.2	94.5
SPADE	3		GT	✓	**23.1**	**26.2**	52.8	50.7
Ours	3		GT	✓ ✓	24.5	29.2	**41.5**	**44.2**
Ours	3		SG	✓ ✓	26.3	39.2	42.9	63.6

Table 2: FID scores (↓) for generated RGB images with varying context and prediction steps, using either ground truth semantics (GT) or Structure Generator predictions (SG) as input.

sults using the semantic images generated by the Structure Generator as inputs (i.e., our full model). To quantify the potential for uplift with better Structure Generators, we also report results using ground truth semantic segmentations as input. We compare to two ablated versions of our model:

- **No Semantics**: The semantic and depth inputs s_t, d_t are removed from the Multi-SPADE blocks.
- **SPADE**: An ablation of the RGB inputs to the model, comprising the previous RGB image I_{t-1} and the re-projected RGB guidance image I'_t. The semantic image s_t replaces I_{t-1} as input to the model and the I'_t input layers are removed from the Multi-SPADE blocks, making this effectively the SPADE model [63].

As shown in Table 2, SPADE performs the best in Val-Seen, indicating that the model has the capacity to memorize the training environments. In this case, RGB inputs are not necessary. However, our model performs noticeably better in Val-Unseen, highlighting the importance of maintaining RGB context in unseen environments (which is our focus). Performance degrades significantly in the No Semantics setting in both Val-Seen and Val-Unseen. We observed that without semantic inputs, the model is unable to generate meaningful images over longer horizons, which

validates our two-stage hierarchical approach. These results are reflected in the FID scores, as well as qualitatively (Figure 6); Image Generator's outputs are significantly crisper, especially over longer horizons. Due to the benefit of guidance images, the Image Generator's textures are also generally better matched with the unseen environment, while SPADE tends to wash out textures, usually creating images of a standard style. Figure 5b plots performance for every setting step-by-step. FID of the Image Generator improves substantially when using ground truth semantics, particularly for longer rollouts, highlighting the potential to benefit from improvements to the Structure Generator.

4.2. VLN Results

Finally, we evaluate whether predictions from Pathdreamer can improve performance on a downstream visual navigation task. We focus on Vision-and-Language Navigation (VLN) using the R2R dataset [3]. Because reaching the navigation goal requires successfully grounding natural language instructions to visual observations, this provides a challenging task-based assessment of prediction quality.

In our inference setting, at each step while moving

Figure 6: Visual comparison of ablated Image Generator outputs on Val-Unseen using *ground truth* segmentation and depth inputs. Both RGB and semantic context is required for best performance.

through the environment we use a baseline VLN agent based on [79] to generate a large number of possible future trajectories using beam search. We then rank these alternative trajectories using an instruction-trajectory compatibility model [84] to assess which trajectory best matches the instruction. The agent then executes the first action from the top-ranked trajectory before repeating the process. We consider three different planning horizons, with future trajectories containing 1, 2 or 3 forward steps.

The instruction-trajectory compatibility model is a dual-encoder that separately encodes textual instructions and trajectories (encoded using visual observations and path geometry) into a shared latent space. To improve performance on incomplete paths, we introduce truncated paths into the original contrastive training scheme proposed in [84]. The compatibility model is trained using only ground truth observations. However, during inference, RGB observations for future steps are drawn from three different sources:

- **Ground truth**: RGB observations from the actual environment, i.e., look-ahead observations.
- **Pathdreamer**: RGB predictions from our model.
- **Repeated pano**: A simple baseline in which the most recent RGB observation is repeated in future steps.

Note that in all cases the geometry of the future trajectories is determined by the ground truth R2R navigation graphs. In Table 3, we report Val-Unseen results for this experiment using standard metrics for VLN: navigation error (NE), success rate (SR), shortest path length (SPL), normalized Dynamic Time Warping (nDTW) [31], and success weighted by normalized Dynamic Time Warping (sDTW) [31].

Consistent with prior work [20, 73], we find that looking ahead using ground truth visual observations provides a robust performance boost, e.g., success rate increases from

Observations	Plan Steps	NE $\downarrow$	SR $\uparrow$	SPL $\uparrow$	nDTW $\uparrow$	sDTW $\uparrow$
Repeated pano	1	6.75	35.7	33.8	52.0	31.2
Pathdreamer	1	6.48	40.3	38.8	55.0	35.6
Ground truth	1	5.80	44.6	42.7	58.9	39.4
Repeated pano	2	6.76	36.8	34.0	51.8	31.7
Pathdreamer	2	5.76	46.5	44.0	59.5	41.0
Ground truth	2	4.95	54.3	51.3	64.9	48.3
Repeated pano	3	6.25	40.6	37.7	55.6	35.2
Pathdreamer	3	5.61	48.9	46.0	60.5	43.1
Ground truth	3	4.44	59.3	55.8	67.9	52.7

Table 3: VLN Val-Unseen results using an instruction-trajectory compatibility model to rank alternative future trajectories with planning horizons of 1, 2 or 3 steps.

44.6% with 1 planning step (top panel) to 59.3% with 3 planning steps (bottom panel). At the other extreme, the Repeated pano baseline is weak, with a success rate of just 35.7% with 1 planning step (top row). This is not surprising: repeating the last pano denies the compatibility model any useful visual representation of the next action, which is crucial to performance [20, 73]. However, increasing the planning horizon does improve performance even for the Repeated pano baseline, since the compatibility model is able to compare the geometry of alternative future trajectories. Finally, we observe that using Pathdreamer's visual observations closes about half the gap between the Repeated pano baseline and the ground truth observations, e.g., 48.9% success with Pathdreamer vs. 40.6% and 59.3% respectively for the others. We conclude that using Pathdreamer as a visual world model can improve performance on downstream tasks, although existing agents still rely on using a navigation graph to define the feasible action space at each step. Pathdreamer is complementary to current SOTA model-based approaches, and a combination would likely lead to further boosts in VLN performance, which is worth investigating in future work.

5. Conclusion

In this paper, we presented Pathdreamer, a stochastic hierarchical visual world model. Pathdreamer is capable of synthesizing realistic and diverse 360° panoramic images for unseen trajectories in real buildings. As a visual world model, Pathdreamer also shows strong promise in improving performance on downstream tasks, such as VLN. Most notably, we show that Pathdreamer captures around half the benefit of looking ahead at actual observations from the environment. The efficacy of Pathdreamer in the VLN task may be attributed to its ability to model fundamental constraints in the real world – relieving the agent from having to learn the geometry and visual and semantic structure of buildings. Applying Pathdreamer to other embodied navigation tasks such as Object-Nav [5], VLN-CE [39] and street-level navigation [9, 53] are natural directions for future work.

References

[1] Sandra Aigner and Marco Körner. Futuregan: Anticipating the future frames of video sequences using spatio-temporal 3d convolutions in progressively growing gans. *arXiv preprint arXiv:1810.01325*, 2018. 2

[2] Peter Anderson, Angel Chang, Devendra Singh Chaplot, Alexey Dosovitskiy, Saurabh Gupta, Vladlen Koltun, Jana Kosecka, Jitendra Malik, Roozbeh Mottaghi, Manolis Savva, and Amir R. Zamir. On evaluation of embodied navigation agents. *arXiv preprint arXiv:1807.06757*, 2018. 3

[3] Peter Anderson, Qi Wu, Damien Teney, Jake Bruce, Mark Johnson, Niko Sünderhauf, Ian Reid, Stephen Gould, and Anton van den Hengel. Vision-and-language navigation: Interpreting visually-grounded navigation instructions in real environments. In *CVPR*, pages 3674–3683, 2018. 1, 2, 3, 5, 6, 7

[4] Mohammad Babaeizadeh, Mohammad Taghi Saffar, Danijar Hafner, Harini Kannan, Chelsea Finn, Sergey Levine, and Dumitru Erhan. Models, pixels, and rewards: Evaluating design trade-offs in visual model-based reinforcement learning. *arXiv preprint arXiv:2012.04603*, 2020. 3

[5] Dhruv Batra, Aaron Gokaslan, Aniruddha Kembhavi, Oleksandr Maksymets, Roozbeh Mottaghi, Manolis Savva, Alexander Toshev, and Erik Wijmans. Objectnav revisited: On evaluation of embodied agents navigating to objects. *arXiv preprint arXiv:2006.13171*, 2020. 1, 3, 8

[6] Lars Buesing, Theophane Weber, Yori Zwols, Sebastien Racaniere, Arthur Guez, Jean-Baptiste Lespiau, and Nicolas Heess. Woulda, coulda, shoulda: Counterfactually-guided policy search. In *ICLR*, 2019. 1

[7] Angel Chang, Angela Dai, Thomas Funkhouser, Maciej Halber, Matthias Niessner, Manolis Savva, Shuran Song, Andy Zeng, and Yinda Zhang. Matterport3d: Learning from RGB-D data in indoor environments. *International Conference on 3D Vision (3DV)*, 2017. 2, 3, 5

[8] Matthew Chang, Arjun Gupta, and Saurabh Gupta. Semantic visual navigation by watching youtube videos. *NeurIPS*, 2020. 3

[9] Howard Chen, Alane Suhr, Dipendra Misra, Noah Snavely, and Yoav Artzi. Touchdown: Natural language navigation and spatial reasoning in visual street environments. In *CVPR*, 2019. 3, 8

[10] Silvia Chiappa, Sébastien Racaniere, Daan Wierstra, and Shakir Mohamed. Recurrent environment simulators. *ICLR*, 2017. 2

[11] Emily Denton and Rob Fergus. Stochastic video generation with a learned prior. 2018. 2, 4

[12] Helisa Dhamo, Keisuke Tateno, Iro Laina, Nassir Navab, and Federico Tombari. Peeking behind objects: Layered depth prediction from a single image. *Pattern Recognition Letters*, 125:333–340, 2019. 3

[13] Alexey Dosovitskiy and Vladlen Koltun. Learning to act by predicting the future. In *ICLR*, 2017. 3

[14] Frederik Ebert, Chelsea Finn, Alex X Lee, and Sergey Levine. Self-supervised visual planning with temporal skip connections. *Conference on Robot Learning (CoRL)*, 2017. 2

[15] Chelsea Finn, Ian Goodfellow, and Sergey Levine. Unsupervised learning for physical interaction through video prediction. In *NeurIPS*, pages 64–72, 2016. 2

[16] Chelsea Finn and Sergey Levine. Deep visual foresight for planning robot motion. In *ICRA*, pages 2786–2793. IEEE, 2017. 1, 2

[17] Chelsea Finn, Xin Yu Tan, Yan Duan, Trevor Darrell, Sergey Levine, and Pieter Abbeel. Deep spatial autoencoders for visuomotor learning. In *ICRA*, pages 512–519. IEEE, 2016. 1

[18] John Flynn, Michael Broxton, Paul Debevec, Matthew DuVall, Graham Fyffe, Ryan Overbeck, Noah Snavely, and Richard Tucker. Deepview: View synthesis with learned gradient descent. In *CVPR*, pages 2367–2376, 2019. 3

[19] John Flynn, Ivan Neulander, James Philbin, and Noah Snavely. Deepstereo: Learning to predict new views from the world's imagery. In *CVPR*, 2016. 1, 3

[20] Daniel Fried, Ronghang Hu, Volkan Cirik, Anna Rohrbach, Jacob Andreas, Louis-Philippe Morency, Taylor Berg-Kirkpatrick, Kate Saenko, Dan Klein, and Trevor Darrell. Speaker-follower models for vision-and-language navigation. *NeurIPS*, 2018. 3, 8

[21] Tsu-Jui Fu, Xin Eric Wang, Matthew F Peterson, Scott T Grafton, Miguel P Eckstein, and William Yang Wang. Counterfactual vision-and-language navigation via adversarial path sampler. In *ECCV*, pages 71–86, 2020. 3

[22] Ian J Goodfellow, Jean Pouget-Abadie, Mehdi Mirza, Bing Xu, David Warde-Farley, Sherjil Ozair, Aaron Courville, and Yoshua Bengio. Generative adversarial networks. *NeurIPS*, 2014. 4

[23] David Ha and Jürgen Schmidhuber. World models. *NeurIPS*, 2018. 1, 2

[24] Danijar Hafner, Timothy Lillicrap, Jimmy Ba, and Mohammad Norouzi. Dream to control: Learning behaviors by latent imagination. *ICLR*, 2019. 2

[25] Danijar Hafner, Timothy Lillicrap, Mohammad Norouzi, and Jimmy Ba. Mastering atari with discrete world models. *arXiv preprint arXiv:2010.02193*, 2020. 1, 2

[26] Meera Hahn, Jacob Krantz, Dhruv Batra, Devi Parikh, James M. Rehg, Stefan Lee, and Peter Anderson. Where are you? localization from embodied dialog. 2020. 1, 3

[27] Weituo Hao, Chunyuan Li, Xiujun Li, Lawrence Carin, and Jianfeng Gao. Towards learning a generic agent for vision-and-language navigation via pre-training. In *CVPR*, June 2020. 3

[28] Kaiming He, Xiangyu Zhang, Shaoqing Ren, and Jian Sun. Deep residual learning for image recognition. In *CVPR*, pages 770–778, 2016. 3

[29] Phlipp Henzler, Volker Rasche, Timo Ropinski, and Tobias Ritschel. Single-image tomography: 3d volumes from 2d cranial x-rays. In *Computer Graphics Forum*, volume 37, pages 377–388. Wiley Online Library, 2018. 3

[30] Martin Heusel, Hubert Ramsauer, Thomas Unterthiner, Bernhard Nessler, and Sepp Hochreiter. GANs trained by a two time-scale update rule converge to a local nash equilibrium. In *NeurIPS*, 2017. 6

[31] Gabriel Ilharco, Vihan Jain, Alexander Ku, Eugene Ie, and Jason Baldridge. General evaluation for instruction conditioned navigation using dynamic time warping. *NeurIPS Workshop on Visually Grounded Interaction and Language (ViGIL)*, 2019. 8

[32] Phillip Isola, Jun-Yan Zhu, Tinghui Zhou, and Alexei A Efros. Image-to-image translation with conditional adversarial networks. *CVPR*, 2017. 5

[33] Vihan Jain, Gabriel Magalhaes, Alexander Ku, Ashish Vaswani, Eugene Ie, and Jason Baldridge. Stay on the path: Instruction fidelity in vision-and-language navigation. 2019. 3

[34] Jindong Jiang, Lunan Zheng, Fei Luo, and Zhijun Zhang. Rednet: Residual encoder-decoder network for indoor rgb-d semantic segmentation. *arXiv preprint arXiv:1806.01054*, 2018. 3

[35] Xiaojie Jin, Huaxin Xiao, Xiaohui Shen, Jimei Yang, Zhe Lin, Yunpeng Chen, Zequn Jie, Jiashi Feng, and Shuicheng Yan. Predicting scene parsing and motion dynamics in the future. In *NeurIPS*, pages 6915–6924, 2017. 2

[36] Justin Johnson, Alexandre Alahi, and Li Fei-Fei. Perceptual losses for real-time style transfer and super-resolution. In *ECCV*, pages 694–711, 2016. 4

[37] Abhishek Kar, Christian Häne, and Jitendra Malik. Learning a multi-view stereo machine. In *NeurIPS*, pages 365–376, 2017. 3

[38] Maximilian Karl, Maximilian Soelch, Justin Bayer, and Patrick Van der Smagt. Deep variational bayes filters: Unsupervised learning of state space models from raw data. *ICLR*, 2017. 2

[39] Jacob Krantz, Erik Wijmans, Arjun Majundar, Dhruv Batra, and Stefan Lee. Beyond the nav-graph: Vision and language navigation in continuous environments. In *ECCV*, 2020. 3, 8

[40] Alexander Ku, Peter Anderson, Roma Patel, Eugene Ie, and Jason Baldridge. Room-across-room: Multilingual vision-and-language navigation with dense spatiotemporal grounding. *EMNLP*, 2020. 1, 3

[41] Yong-Hoon Kwon and Min-Gyu Park. Predicting future frames using retrospective cycle gan. In *CVPR*, pages 1811–1820, 2019. 2

[42] Wonkwang Lee, Whie Jung, Han Zhang, Ting Chen, Jing Yu Koh, Thomas Huang, Hyungsuk Yoon, Honglak Lee, and Seunghoon Hong. Revisiting hierarchical approach for persistent long-term video prediction. In *ICLR*, 2021. 2, 6

[43] Zuoyue Li, Zhaopeng Cui, and Martin R Oswald. Streetview panoramic video synthesis from a single satellite image. *arXiv preprint arXiv:2012.06628*, 2020. 2

[44] Andrew Liu, Richard Tucker, Varun Jampani, Ameesh Makadia, Noah Snavely, and Angjoo Kanazawa. Infinite nature: Perpetual view generation of natural scenes from a single image. *arXiv preprint arXiv:2012.09855*, 2020. 2

[45] Guilin Liu, Fitsum A Reda, Kevin J Shih, Ting-Chun Wang, Andrew Tao, and Bryan Catanzaro. Image inpainting for irregular holes using partial convolutions. In *ECCV*, pages 85–100, 2018. 4

[46] Jiasen Lu, Dhruv Batra, Devi Parikh, and Stefan Lee. Vilbert: Pretraining task-agnostic visiolinguistic representations for vision-and-language tasks. In *NeurIPS*, pages 13–23, 2019. 3

[47] Pauline Luc, Natalia Neverova, Camille Couprie, Jakob Verbeek, and Yann LeCun. Predicting deeper into the future of semantic segmentation. In *ICCV*, pages 648–657, 2017. 2

[48] Chih-Yao Ma, Jiasen Lu, Zuxuan Wu, Ghassan AlRegib, Zsolt Kira, Richard Socher, and Caiming Xiong. Self-monitoring navigation agent via auxiliary progress estimation. *ICLR*, 2019. 3

[49] Chih-Yao Ma, Zuxuan Wu, Ghassan AlRegib, Caiming Xiong, and Zsolt Kira. The regretful agent: Heuristic-aided navigation through progress estimation. In *CVPR*, pages 6732–6740, 2019. 3

[50] Arjun Majumdar, Ayush Shrivastava, Stefan Lee, Peter Anderson, Devi Parikh, and Dhruv Batra. Improving vision-and-language navigation with image-text pairs from the web. *ECCV*, 2020. 2, 3

[51] Arun Mallya, Ting-Chun Wang, Karan Sapra, and Ming-Yu Liu. World-consistent video-to-video synthesis. *ECCV*, 2020. 2, 3, 4

[52] Ricardo Martin-Brualla, Noha Radwan, Mehdi S. M. Sajjadi, Jonathan T. Barron, Alexey Dosovitskiy, and Daniel Duckworth. NeRF in the Wild: Neural Radiance Fields for Unconstrained Photo Collections. In *CVPR*, 2021. 3

[53] Harsh Mehta, Yoav Artzi, Jason Baldridge, Eugene Ie, and Piotr Mirowski. Retouchdown: Adding touchdown to streetlearn as a shareable resource for language grounding tasks in street view. *EMNLP Workshop on Spatial Language Understanding (SpLU)*, 2020. 3, 8

[54] Ben Mildenhall, Pratul P Srinivasan, Rodrigo Ortiz-Cayon, Nima Khademi Kalantari, Ravi Ramamoorthi, Ren Ng, and Abhishek Kar. Local light field fusion: Practical view synthesis with prescriptive sampling guidelines. *ACM Transactions on Graphics (TOG)*, 38(4):1–14, 2019. 3

[55] Ben Mildenhall, Pratul P Srinivasan, Matthew Tancik, Jonathan T Barron, Ravi Ramamoorthi, and Ren Ng. Nerf: Representing scenes as neural radiance fields for view synthesis. *ECCV*, 2020. 3

[56] Piotr Mirowski, Andras Banki-Horvath, Keith Anderson, Denis Teplyashin, Karl Moritz Hermann, Mateusz Malinowski, Matthew Koichi Grimes, Karen Simonyan, Koray Kavukcuoglu, Andrew Zisserman, et al. The streetlearn environment and dataset. *arXiv preprint arXiv:1903.01292*, 2019. 3

[57] Anusha Nagabandi, Gregory Kahn, Ronald S Fearing, and Sergey Levine. Neural network dynamics for model-based deep reinforcement learning with model-free fine-tuning. In *ICRA*, pages 7559–7566. IEEE, 2018. 1

[58] Medhini Narasimhan, Erik Wijmans, Xinlei Chen, Trevor Darrell, Dhruv Batra, Devi Parikh, and Amanpreet Singh. Seeing the un-scene: Learning amodal semantic maps for room navigation. In *ECCV*, pages 513–529. Springer, 2020. 3

[59] Khanh Nguyen and Hal Daumé III. Help, anna! visual navigation with natural multimodal assistance via retrospective curiosity-encouraging imitation learning. *EMNLP*, 2019. 3

[60] Junhyuk Oh, Xiaoxiao Guo, Honglak Lee, Richard L Lewis, and Satinder Singh. Action-conditional video prediction using deep networks in atari games. In *NeurIPS*, pages 2863–2871, 2015. 2

[61] Junhyuk Oh, Satinder Singh, and Honglak Lee. Value prediction network. In I. Guyon, U. V. Luxburg, S. Bengio, H. Wallach, R. Fergus, S. Vishwanathan, and R. Garnett, editors, *NeurIPS*, 2017. 3

[62] Blazej Osinski, Chelsea Finn, Dumitru Erhan, George Tucker, Henryk Michalewski, Konrad Czechowski, Lukasz Mieczyslaw Kaiser, Mohammad Babaeizadeh, Piotr Kozakowski, Piotr Milos, Roy H Campbell, Afroz Mohiuddin, Ryan Sepassi, and Sergey Levine. Model-based reinforcement learning for atari. In *ICLR*, 2020. 1, 2

[63] Taesung Park, Ming-Yu Liu, Ting-Chun Wang, and Jun-Yan Zhu. Semantic image synthesis with spatially-adaptive normalization. In *CVPR*, pages 2337–2346, 2019. 2, 4, 5, 7

[64] Aj Piergiovanni, Alan Wu, and Michael S Ryoo. Learning real-world robot policies by dreaming. In *IEEE/RSJ International Conference on Intelligent Robots and Systems (IROS)*, pages 7680–7687. IEEE, 2019. 1

[65] Senthil Purushwalkam, Sebastian Vicenc Amengual Gari, Vamsi Krishna Ithapu, Carl Schissler, Philip Robinson, Abhinav Gupta, and Kristen Grauman. Audio-visual floorplan reconstruction. *arXiv preprint arXiv:2012.15470*, 2020. 3

[66] Yuankai Qi, Qi Wu, Peter Anderson, Xin Wang, William Yang Wang, Chunhua Shen, and Anton van den Hengel. Reverie: Remote embodied visual referring expression in real indoor environments. In *CVPR*, 2020. 1, 3

[67] Manolis Savva, Abhishek Kadian, Oleksandr Maksymets, Yili Zhao, Erik Wijmans, Bhavana Jain, Julian Straub, Jia Liu, Vladlen Koltun, Jitendra Malik, Devi Parikh, and Dhruv Batra. Habitat: A Platform for Embodied AI Research. In *ICCV*, 2019. 5

[68] Meng-Li Shih, Shih-Yang Su, Johannes Kopf, and Jia-Bin Huang. 3d photography using context-aware layered depth inpainting. In *CVPR*, June 2020. 3

[69] Karen Simonyan and Andrew Zisserman. Very deep convolutional networks for large-scale image recognition. *ICLR*, 2015. 4

[70] Pratul P Srinivasan, Richard Tucker, Jonathan T Barron, Ravi Ramamoorthi, Ren Ng, and Noah Snavely. Pushing the boundaries of view extrapolation with multiplane images. In *CVPR*, pages 175–184, 2019. 3

[71] Julian Straub, Thomas Whelan, Lingni Ma, Yufan Chen, Erik Wijmans, Simon Green, Jakob J. Engel, Raul Mur-Artal, Carl Ren, Shobhit Verma, Anton Clarkson, Mingfei Yan, Brian Budge, Yajie Yan, Xiaqing Pan, June Yon, Yuyang Zou, Kimberly Leon, Nigel Carter, Jesus Briales, Tyler Gillingham, Elias Mueggler, Luis Pesqueira, Manolis Savva, Dhruv Batra, Hauke M. Strasdat, Renzo De Nardi, Michael Goesele, Steven Lovegrove, and Richard Newcombe. The Replica dataset: A digital replica of indoor spaces. *arXiv preprint arXiv:1906.05797*, 2019. 3

[72] Richard S. Sutton and Andrew G. Barto. *Reinforcement Learning: An Introduction*. A Bradford Book, Cambridge, MA, USA, 2018. 1

[73] Hao Tan, Licheng Yu, and Mohit Bansal. Learning to navigate unseen environments: Back translation with environmental dropout. In *Proceedings of the 2019 Conference of the North American Chapter of the Association for Computational Linguistics: Human Language Technologies, Volume 1 (Long and Short Papers)*, pages 2610–2621, 2019. 3, 8

[74] Jesse Thomason, Michael Murray, Maya Cakmak, and Luke Zettlemoyer. Vision-and-dialog navigation. In *Conference on Robot Learning (CoRL)*, pages 394–406. PMLR, 2020. 1, 3

[75] Suhani Vora, Reza Mahjourian, Soeren Pirk, and Anelia Angelova. Future semantic segmentation leveraging 3d information. *ECCV 3D Reconstruction meets Semantics Workshop*, 2018. 2

[76] Jacob Walker, Abhinav Gupta, and Martial Hebert. Patch to the future: Unsupervised visual prediction. In *CVPR*, pages 3302–3309, 2014. 2

[77] Ting-Chun Wang, Ming-Yu Liu, Jun-Yan Zhu, Guilin Liu, Andrew Tao, Jan Kautz, and Bryan Catanzaro. Video-to-video synthesis. *NeurIPS*, 2018. 2

[78] Ting-Chun Wang, Ming-Yu Liu, Jun-Yan Zhu, Andrew Tao, Jan Kautz, and Bryan Catanzaro. High-resolution image synthesis and semantic manipulation with conditional gans. In *CVPR*, pages 8798–8807, 2018. 4

[79] Xin Wang, Qiuyuan Huang, Asli Celikyilmaz, Jianfeng Gao, Dinghan Shen, Yuan-Fang Wang, William Yang Wang, and Lei Zhang. Reinforced cross-modal matching and self-supervised imitation learning for vision-language navigation. In *CVPR*, pages 6629–6638, 2019. 8

[80] Olivia Wiles, Georgia Gkioxari, Richard Szeliski, and Justin Johnson. Synsin: End-to-end view synthesis from a single image. In *CVPR*, pages 7467–7477, 2020. 1, 3

[81] Fei Xia, Amir R. Zamir, Zhi-Yang He, Alexander Sax, Jitendra Malik, and Silvio Savarese. Gibson env: real-world perception for embodied agents. In *CVPR*. IEEE, 2018. 3

[82] Jingwei Xu, Bingbing Ni, Zefan Li, Shuo Cheng, and Xiaokang Yang. Structure preserving video prediction. In *CVPR*, pages 1460–1469, 2018. 2

[83] Alex Yu, Vickie Ye, Matthew Tancik, and Angjoo Kanazawa. pixelnerf: Neural radiance fields from one or few images. *arXiv preprint arXiv:2012.02190*, 2020. 3

[84] Ming Zhao, Peter Anderson, Vihan Jain, Su Wang, Alex Ku, Jason Baldridge, and Eugene Ie. On the evaluation of vision-and-language navigation instructions. In *Conference of the European Chapter of the Association for Computational Linguistics (EACL)*, 2021. 8

[85] Tinghui Zhou, Richard Tucker, John Flynn, Graham Fyffe, and Noah Snavely. Stereo magnification: Learning view synthesis using multiplane images. *SIGGRAPH*, 2018. 3

[86] Fengda Zhu, Yi Zhu, Xiaojun Chang, and Xiaodan Liang. Vision-language navigation with self-supervised auxiliary reasoning tasks. In *CVPR*, pages 10012–10022, 2020. 3

[87] Wanrong Zhu, Xin Wang, Tsu-Jui Fu, An Yan, Pradyumna Narayana, Kazoo Sone, Sugato Basu, and William Yang Wang. Multimodal text style transfer for outdoor vision-and-language navigation. *EACL*, 2021. 3

Author Index